PENGUIN BOOKS

Little Boy Lost

Little Boy Lost

SHANE DUNPHY

PENGUIN BOOKS

PENGUIN BOOKS

Published by the Penguin Group
Penguin Books Ltd, 80 Strand, London WC2R ORL, England
Penguin Group (USA) Inc., 375 Hudson Street, New York, New York 10014, USA
Penguin Group (Canada), 90 Eglinton Avenue East, Suite 700, Toronto, Ontario, Canada M4P 2Y3
(a division of Pearson Penguin Canada Inc.)
Penguin Ireland, 25 St Stephen's Green, Dublin 2, Ireland (a division of Penguin Books Ltd)
Penguin Group (Australia), 250 Camberwell Road, Camberwell, Victoria 3124, Australia
(a division of Pearson Australia Group Pty Ltd)
Penguin Books India Pvt Ltd, 11 Community Centre, Panchsheel Park, New Delhi – 110 017, India
Penguin Group (NZ), 67 Apollo Drive, Rosedale, North Shore 0632, New Zealand
(a division of Pearson New Zealand Ltd)
Penguin Books (South Africa) (Pty) Ltd, 24 Sturdee Avenue,
Rosebank, Johannesburg 2196, South Africa

Penguin Books Ltd, Registered Offices: 80 Strand, London WC2R ORL, England

www.penguin.com

First published 2009
1

NOTE: *The names of people and places mentioned in this book have been
changed where it was felt necessary to protect the identity of individuals*

Typeset by Rowland Phototypesetting Ltd, Bury St Edmunds, Suffolk
Printed in England by Clays Ltd, St Ives plc

ISBN: 978-1-844-88212-0

www.greenpenguin.co.uk

Penguin Books is committed to a sustainable future
for our business, our readers and our planet.
The book in your hands is made from paper
certified by the Forest Stewardship Council.

For Derek, who taught me that life is sometimes just
about singing your favourite song.

For Leigh, who went out of her way to spread the word.

And for Marty, who somehow understands where
I'm coming from better than most.

Oh Lordy me, and oh, Lordy my:
Especially when you haven't got a dime;
Your troubles get so deep, that you can't hardly sleep.
Then you'll know you've troubles just like mine . . .

Traditional folk song from
the singing of Kilby Snow

Prologue

I think of him almost daily, which is strange, as I have worked with so many others over many years, yet he remains vivid in my memory, like a mental tattoo. I can hear his voice clearly when I close my eyes: I remember him singing, his head to one side as he crooned in a rich, tuneful voice a corny country song; I recall the odd things he would say, the strange juxtapositions of words, always at the wrong time, accompanied by a bubbling laugh that always made me laugh despite myself. I see him standing among the group on the first day I met him, a foot taller than me with an athlete's build and a face startling in its beauty, but with something missing behind the eyes – a subtle disconnect that made him seem a little off-kilter.

His name was Dominic. He was a simple gentle soul, a young man damaged by fate, who had been left with a child's view of the world; a person for whom joy and sadness flitted across the plain of his heart with sometimes frightening rapidity. Each was grasped and experienced with alarming intensity and with total acceptance. For Dominic, life was something to be experienced in the moment. It would have been easy to assume that this boy spent his life in a fog of muddled misunderstanding, but such a supposition would have been completely inaccurate: for Dominic, life was all about certainties. Dominic was a person of absolutes.

Yet for all that, the time I spent with him was one of the most confused of my career in child protection – I was lost and wounded, and had set out alone to find a path I recognized. When that path presented itself, Dominic was already on it, and with him were others who, selflessly, chose to help guide me on my way. Their stories are intertwined with his, and at times take precedence in the narrative; yet it is Dominic who is central to everything that happened that year – he is the fulcrum upon which everything else was balanced.

So I think of him, and despite myself, I smile. Looking back, it is perhaps strange that the story does not, in fact, begin with Dominic at all. It starts with a beautiful girl and a misplaced fifty euro note.

PART I

Stranger in a Strange Land

Nought loves another as itself
Nor venerates another so.
Nor is it possible to thought
A greater than itself to know.

And Father, how can I love you,
Or any of my brothers more?
I love you like the little bird
That picks up crumbs around the door.

From 'A Little Boy Lost' by
William Blake

I

The first time I saw her, she was standing on the street outside the Ragged Fox pub, in the village of Drumalogue, in the midlands. The light of a streetlamp caught her dark hair and made it shimmer, and her brown eyes flashed with fun and mischief. She was beautiful, and the strange old-fashioned clothes she wore did little to hide her slender yet curvaceous figure. I glanced at her appreciatively as I went past – she was probably twenty-five or twenty-six years old, and I could see that she had the attention of several other young men from the bar, too. A small chip shop nestled beside the Ragged Fox on Drumalogue's short thoroughfare, and a few small groups of people were hanging around outside, eating from grease-stained paper or smoking. One man, obviously the alpha male of his clique, approached the smiling, laughing-eyed girl, and whispered something into her ear.

It was after closing time on a Thursday night in May, and as I packed my instruments into the deceptively spacious boot of my ancient Austin, I experienced that peaceful contentment I always get after a gig has gone well. And the gig that night had gone very well, indeed: the audience had been attentive and enthusiastic in their applause and encouragement, my fingers had found the chords and melodies with ease, and my voice had reached every note I tried for. I had money in my pocket, and further performances booked for every night over the coming weekend – life, just then, was good.

It had been eighteen months since I had left the city and my job as a child protection worker with the Dunleavy Trust, a voluntary group which specialized in working with children in the most difficult of circumstances. Initially, the change of location – and pace – had been difficult to cope with. Several times a day I had found myself reaching for my mobile phone to call Ben Tyrrell, my old boss, to ask for my job back.

But I had made my decision, and was determined to make things work. My last case at Dunleavy House, involving a boy I had worked with many years before (and had failed utterly), had caused me to re-evaluate how my life was going, and how I felt about my career. I knew I needed a break, and the only way to really make that happen was to get out of the city I called home once and for all. Every street corner, each set of traffic lights, all the faces, known and unknown, carried memories for me, and for a clean break to occur, I had to get away from it all.

I had lived in the midlands as a community childcare worker several years earlier, and had enjoyed it. There was a place, covering around thirty square miles and taking in the borders of three counties, which had a small village at the centre of it and little else, and I picked it to make my home. I felt a power-ful desire to be alone, to lose myself in open space, and to reconnect with who I was. I planned to read and perhaps to write, to walk and to think. I determined to make my living as a musician and get a job cooking or washing dishes if that didn't work out.

Getting work playing music turned out to be the easy part. I put together a set list of well-known Irish ballads, and threw in some slightly more unusual American and English tunes. I play enough instruments to keep my sound interesting, and a one-night stand in one of the local pubs led to a Wednesday night residency there, which in turn caught the interest of several other landlords. Within a month, I was turning work down.

So it was that I was at the Ragged Fox that Thursday night when this girl – seemingly from another time – gambolled into my life. Having finished squaring away my gear, I closed the boot, and leaned against the side of the car, counting my wages. It was then I realized I had fifty euro too much. As a working musician, I was sorely tempted to pocket this unexpected windfall and drive off into the night. However, I had enjoyed playing in the pub, and had been promised further nights there. If I conned the management, it was unlikely such gigs would take place. I decided it would be better to go back inside and point out the error.

As I made my way to the front door, I heard a scuffle, and a loud cry of anger, followed by bubbling laughter. Turning, I saw the oddly dressed girl sprawled in the road, still laughing manically, with the young buck who had been attempting to woo her standing over her fallen figure threateningly.

'You fucking sick bitch,' he said, drawing his leg back to kick her.

'Hey,' I said, unsettled by what I was witnessing. 'Why don't you cool it?'

I was acutely aware that I was surrounded by locals, and that in any fracas I would be considered the outsider, a fact which would most likely result in my receiving a sound beating. But this girl was completely alone. I could not stand by and watch her be manhandled. I placed myself between the angry man and the object of his wrath, who was still giggling like a small child.

'This ain't your business, lad,' the man, said, peering over my shoulder at his prey. 'She's got a hidin' comin', and I'm the fella to give it to her.'

'Half a pound of tuppenny rice, half a pound of treacle,' the girl sang behind me. 'That's the way the money goes . . .'

'I think she's just had too much to drink,' I said. 'Why don't you cut her some slack?'

'*Pop!* Goes the weasel,' the prone girl sang, clapping her hands at the 'Pop!' and giggling some more.

The young man's friends had gathered tightly round us, expecting things might escalate between me and their compatriot. He had stopped trying to get at the girl, and was now looking at her with something akin to disgust and pity.

'I think she's fuckin' stoned, Gully,' one of the group said, as the weird creature began a strange, skipping, weaving dance in the centre of the melee.

The man who was before me scowled, and turned away. 'She's not worth the hassle,' he said, and then to me, 'and neither are you.'

He stalked off, and the crowd of stragglers slowly followed. The girl continued her childlike dance in the road, accompanying her movements with a falsetto sing-song that had no words I could discern. I stood and watched her for a moment. No one was bothering her by then; the final late drinkers from the bar were moving off. I could see the woman behind the counter in the chipper beginning to wipe down the counter and shut off the deep-fat fryer. There was very little traffic around. I knew I could leave her, and she would more than likely not come to any immediate harm.

I took a few steps towards the partially open door of the Ragged Fox, determined just to give the landlord back his money, and then get out of there. I had a bottle of good whiskey at the cottage I was renting; I was reading Neil Gaiman's *Coraline* and was looking forward to returning to it. I'd had a vision of lighting a small fire, putting Bob Dylan's *Desire* on the stereo (I had a copy in vinyl, which I firmly believe sounds much better than any CD) and spending a couple of hours reading and winding down before bed.

This peculiar damsel in distress was a most unwanted distraction.

By the time I got to the door of the pub, her off-key warblings had inserted themselves firmly into my consciousness and I could ignore her no more. I stood and watched her for a moment, exasperated, every grain of common sense telling me just to walk away. Sighing deeply, however, I walked slowly back to where she danced, and gently placed a hand on her shoulder.

'Hey,' I said, keeping my voice as soft and neutral as I could.

By this time, I knew the girl was either intellectually disabled or was having some kind of psychiatric breakdown. 'Are you all on your own? Is your mum or dad around?'

My hand prevented her from moving in the loose circle she had been navigating, but she continued to sway in time to music I could not hear. She was certainly aware I was there, but she did not look at me, or try to communicate.

'What's your name, sweetheart?' I tried again. 'I'm Shane —'

'You're wastin' your time with that one,' a voice cut across me. 'She's touched, so she is. You'll not get much good out of her.'

Douglas, the landlord of the Ragged Fox, was bringing in the blackboard he always left hanging outside the front door on which he wrote the short menu of food — mostly soups and sandwiches — he sold every day.

'She seems lost,' I said. 'Are her parents about? A brother or sister, maybe?'

Douglas tutted and shook his head. 'As far as I know, her family are all as daft as she is. Leave her where she is. She'll make her own way home.'

'Where does she live?'

'Up on the mountain.'

'The mountain?'

'Aye.'

'But that's what . . . six, seven miles from here.'

'S'right.'

'We can't let her walk that at this hour of the night.'

Douglas was a short, balding man, with a spectacular beer gut that protruded over the short apron he wore and made the buttons on the front of his shirt look as if they might pop off like miniature cannonballs at any moment. He shook his head in annoyance.

'Oh, you'd better bring her in. When I've cleaned the place up, we'll drop her out home.'

I began to lead the girl gently towards the pub. 'Thanks, Doug. I appreciate it.'

'You can keep her amused, though,' the man warned. 'She can be a right feckin' handful, and I won't have her running riot about my premises.'

'I'll see what I can manage,' I said, and changed direction to retrieve my autoharp from the boot of the Austin. With this slung over my shoulder, I led the still uncommunicative girl into the bar.

She seemed to have almost shut down; her eyes were open, but there was little going on behind them. I thought, with sickening certainty, that I could do whatsoever I wished with this odd woman/child, and she would offer little resistance. My mind turned again to the gang outside, and I knew I had been right to intercede when I had. I didn't want to think about what could have happened had I not.

I sat my charge down near the door, and pulled another chair over so that I was sitting opposite. I flipped open the case of the autoharp, chatting to her as I went.

'What's your name, hon?'

She was looking at me now very intently.

'What's dat?' she asked all of a sudden, motioning with a hand at the instrument I was unpacking.

'This is an autoharp,' I said, sitting it across my knees.

The autoharp is an odd instrument, kind of a cross between a guitar, a harp and an accordion. Technically, it's called a chorded zither. Made from polished wood (mine is in a kind of dark sunburst), and roughly rectangularly shaped, the autoharp has thirty-eight strings, each tuned to a different note. Mine has twenty-one buttons, which, when pressed down, cause a bar to lower onto the strings, dampening all the notes not in the chord you want to play. It has a sweet, jangling sound, and lends itself well to American and English folk songs. I have adapted it to some Irish ballads, too.

I had thought that the unusual nature of the instrument

might capture her attention, and give me an inroad into what she was doing all on her own so far from home.

'Listen,' I said, and strummed the chord of G for her.

'Oh,' she said, catching her breath.

She reached out, and touched the strings tentatively, as if she was afraid they might bite her.

'What's your name, sweetie?' I asked again.

'Name?'

'Yeah. I'm Shane.' I lifted her chin gently so she was looking at me. 'Shane,' I repeated, patting my chest for emphasis as I said it. 'What is *your* name?'

'Shane,' she said, very gently strumming the autoharp with the tips of her fingers. I noticed that, despite the fact her dress was very worn and faded, she was scrupulously clean. Her hair shone, and her nails were clipped and spotless. She smelt of soap and fresh air.

'That's right. I'm Shane. And you are . . .'

'You are . . .'

I gave up.

'Will we sing?' I asked her.

'Yeah!'

'What shall we sing, then?'

The girl just looked at me, smiling blankly.

'Sing,' she said again.

'Okay,' I said. 'You sing this after me, then.'

I tried an old American call and answer song, thinking it might suit my audience best.

Oh, Eliza, li'l Liza Jane!
Oh, Eliza, li'l Liza Jane!

I tried it again, and the second time, she mimicked me perfectly. I went through it a few more times, then tried a verse, punctuating each line with the refrain: Li'l Liza Jane.

I know a gal that you don't know,
(Li'l Liza Jane!),
Lives in the mountains where the flowers grow.
(Li'l Li-za Jane!).

She joined in, clapping her hands in delight as we sang, swaying from side to side in rhythm with the punchy beat.

Liza Jane looks good to me
(Li'l Liza Jane!),
Prettiest girl I ever did see,
(Li'l Liza Jane!)

When the song finished, she bounced on her chair like a small child, and proclaimed: 'Again, again.'

This time, I could hear Douglas joining in on the callbacks, and had to smile to myself as he whisked past us, sweeping the floor in time to the old song.

It wasn't long before the stools were upside down on the bar, and Douglas was switching off the lights. 'Come on then, have ye no homes to go to?' he said, echoing the eternal lament of the publican.

'Will that thing make it up into the sticks?' my companion asked when he had the front door locked and we were standing by my car.

'Only had her serviced a week ago.'

'I didn't ask you that.'

'It'll make it. She drives like a dream.'

'Okay then. Let's go. Sooner we go, sooner we'll be back.'

The girl, whom I was starting to think of as Liza, after the song (and, indeed, the name had an old-fashioned quality that seemed to suit her), climbed into the back seat without having to be told, and promptly fell asleep. I started the engine, and turned north towards the dark shape of Mount Muireann looming above the village out of the night.

'So tell me about our friend, then,' I said as the road coiled out ahead like a blue ribbon.

'Not much to tell,' Douglas said. 'Everyone hereabouts knows her people. They're a quare bunch, living up in the highlands in a kind of shack – barely civilized at all. From what I've been told, they used to own a farm up there, but those goats and sheep run pretty much wild now, and there's no fields you could grow anything on any more in them parts. I don't know how they feed themselves – welfare, I s'pose.'

'Is Liza there on her own?'

'How'd'you mean?'

'Are there many of them in it? Does she look after elderly parents or what?'

'Does *she* look after her parents? Sure, she's like a small babby.'

'I used to work with people like her in another life, Douglas. I've seen children who were little more than toddlers take care of alcoholic or drug-addicted parents. You'd be amazed what kids can do if they have to.'

He grunted assent. 'You're right, I reckon. I've had little 'uns coming into the bar to collect their dads and mams on dole day, more or less takin' the money out of their hands to buy food. It's one of the hard things, in my business, to have to witness that.'

It occurred to me that Douglas didn't have to keep serving such people when he knew their children were at home, unsupervised and hungry, but I kept the thought to myself. The ethics of working in a bar had never been something I'd had to contend with, so I gave him the benefit of the doubt.

'So does she have any brothers or sisters? Are they all intellectually disabled?'

'I think there might be another couple of kids in it, all right, but as far as I know they're all like her, and the parents, who are about my age' – Douglas was in his sixties, I guessed – 'are mighty strange, and that's putting it kindly. The dad, William, now I knew him from school. He used come in the odd time, with the arse out of his trousers and no shoes on his feet, wild and skinny and barely able to scratch out his name. We used to give him a fierce hard time, but, sure, you know what kids are like. He was the class hard-luck case, and we all knew it. Turn left up here.'

The lane was overhung with trees and bushes, and huge potholes made the going treacherous. I slowed to a bare crawl.

'It's just up a little bit ahead now. You'll be on it before you know,' Douglas warned me.

Sure enough, suddenly, the side of a rough stone wall – part of a larger building that disappeared into the shrubbery on the left-hand side of the lane – protruded halfway out into the crude roadway, making it impossible to pass. I realized in a rush that I would have to reverse all the way back to the main road, and mentally cursed Douglas for not warning me; with all the blind corners, it would be a difficult return trip.

I turned to look at our sleeping passenger. She was deeply unconscious, breathing steadily and regularly.

'Hey,' I said, shaking her gently. 'You're home, Liza.'

Like a child being woken for school, the girl rolled over and showed me a pointed shoulder.

'She's not goin' anywhere in a hurry,' Douglas said, rolling down the window and taking a pack of non-filter cigarettes from his breast pocket.

I opened the door and climbed out, to lift her physically if necessary. A few more gentle shakes and she was sitting up, blinking in the semi-darkness.

'You have to go home now, hon,' I said. 'Do you have a key to get in?'

'Home . . .' she repeated, and struggled out into the night air.

'We have company,' Douglas said sharply.

'Daddy,' Liza said, and I saw the man who was now standing in the grim laneway, in the full headlights of the Austin.

He was tall, probably six foot four or five, and dressed in what looked like ancient overalls, which were so dirty and discoloured they had taken on a kind of generic grey hue. His hair was a greasy tangle of white with a yellow tinge, and on his feet were the most enormous pair of hobnailed boots I had ever seen. His face was a mask of anger and bewilderment. His eyes – piggish and too close together – were squinting against the light, and his chin was obscured by thick white stubble. I couldn't tell if he was fat or heavily muscled, but I got the sense of huge bulk, behind which I knew would be a powerful strength.

There was no doubt in my mind that he saw us as intruders. He did not look one bit happy.

'Daddy,' Liza said again, but I was aware that, rather than moving towards the man who was obviously her father, she was pressing back against me with no little force.

'Umm,' I said, feeling strongly that I should say something at this point, 'we're just leaving your daughter home, sir. She was down in Drumalogue, and we didn't feel it was safe for her to walk home so late.'

The man lowered his gaze to the girl.

'You run off again, child,' he said, his voice a low and guttural growl.

Liza did not answer.

'You go on to your bed now,' he said, and turned and disappeared into the darkness. I could hear his huge frame moving through the foliage that hung down into the laneway for some long moments. Liza hung back until she was sure he was gone, then she shot off round the corner of the old building, leaving me standing in the night.

'Can I go home now?' Douglas asked. 'Some of us have businesses to run.'

'Uh – yeah, okay. I'm coming,' I said.

'Well, are you satisfied?' my companion asked when I finally managed to get us back on the road and was pointed for home.

'In what way?'

'Well, you rescued the maiden in distress. Did you get a word of thanks? Did old William shake your hand and praise you for bringing his wee girl home safe? Do you feel that your efforts were appreciated?'

'No,' I admitted. 'None of those things happened.'

'Waste of time then, wasn't it?' Douglas said, sounding pleased at the declaration.

I lit a cigarette of my own from the dashboard lighter.

'I would not have slept properly tonight, knowing that little girl was wandering about, at risk from any arsehole who happened upon her. I know she's home now, and that's a relief.'

Douglas nodded, watching the ditches and scrub that sped past.

'I see. And you're not going to toss and turn, wondering just how safe she is in that shit hole we just left her in, with that ogre of a man?'

I said nothing to that. I had a feeling sleep was many hours away.

Douglas refused to take the money when I left him back at the bar. I thanked him and drove towards my home amid the fields and the hedgerows, wondering about Liza, and why she had come out of the mountains to find me.

2

Over the next two weeks I thought often of Liza, but on each occasion I pushed the questions and concerns that occurred to me to the back of my mind, and got on with the new life I had made for myself.

My cottage, a simple one-bedroom affair, had been built as a labourer's residence in the early nineteenth century and needed some maintenance, and although I am spectacularly unskilled in such basic practicalities, I bought some tools and DIY manuals, and threw myself into the tasks wholeheartedly. To my surprise, the results were not at all bad: the door I rehung fitted its frame snugly, the drain I unblocked remained free-flowing, and the guttering I cleared and then repaired did not fall from the roof.

Proud of myself, I sought permission from the landlord (an old farmer who was delighted with the few euros rent I paid) to plant some vegetables in the back garden. He not only agreed, but offered to contribute to the project by giving me some potato tubers and young cabbages – the traditional crops of that part of the country – to get me started.

My new benefactor, whose name was Joss, proved to be a firm yet patient teacher, who took great pleasure in sitting on an old stone offering suggestions as I turned over, stoned, weeded and raked the small patch of earth which was to be my new vegetable garden.

'It's all about giving the soil space to breathe,' he informed me, a short black briar pipe clenched between his teeth, a wisp of tobacco smoke twirling about his ear. 'You need to treat the earth tenderly. If you want her to give you food, then you have to woo her, like a woman.'

'Like a woman. Got it,' I grunted, beating a sod apart with my fork, and pulling the grass that sat atop it out by the roots.

'People have no respect for the land,' Joss continued. His lessons were always punctuated by musings on the nature of modern agriculture. 'It's all pesticides and crop quotas and feckin' land taxes . . . how the hell is a soul to make any class of a living out of it any more?'

'You've got me there, Joss,' I said, picking the sharp flinty stones from the newly exposed patch of dark soil.

'It can't be done,' he said, as if I hadn't spoken. 'The small farmer is at a severe disadvantage. I tell you, what you're about is the best way to do it. You're beholden to nobody, and you can have the pleasure of growing something you planted and tended yourself, without having to give the men in suits their pound of flesh.'

We continued in this vein for another hour or so, until Joss decided it was time for tea. He was always acutely aware of the need to keep me hydrated with liberal dosings of strong tea during my horticultural tutelage. He had also discovered that I baked a good scone, and was always happy to sample one or two when visiting. 'There's no shame in a man being able to cook well,' he informed me. 'When I was a lad, a man was expected to be able to darn his own socks and make a pot of stew if called upon to do so. I always thought it a scandal, them fellas who'd nearly starve if their wives went away for a day or so. Soft eejits.'

I set the old copper kettle on the hob to boil, only to discover on investigation that I was out of milk. I drink tea and coffee black, and often forget to restock my fridge in case of visitors.

'I have to pop into town to get some milk, Joss,' I informed my guest. 'You'll be okay for a few minutes?'

'For certain. I'll pull a few more weeds out while you're away. Have you e'er a bit of jam for the scones?'

'I do.'

'And butter?'

16

'In plenty. I'll just be ten minutes, Joss.'

'Right you are.'

I was leaving the village shop, a litre of milk and the morning paper under my arm, when I heard a tuneless voice raised in song, 'Oh, Eliza, li'l Liza Jane!'

I stopped dead in my tracks, and looked about to find the source of the off-key singing. I knew there could only be one person who knew those words, although I was amazed that she had remembered them.

'How many nickels does it take? Li'l Liza Jane! To take you sailin' on the lake? Li'l Liza Jane!'

At last I spotted her. The girl was in a group of young adults – there were maybe ten of them – walking along the footpath across the road from where I stood. I could see that they were all, at varying levels, intellectually disabled (they were linking arms, and two among the group clearly had Down's Syndrome), and I could easily pick out the three carers who were shepherding them along the path. Without hesitation, I jogged over. Liza saw me coming, and laughed giddily, breaking free from the line and rushing over.

'Sing, sing!' she said. She picked up the arm that wasn't holding groceries and turned it over, then looked behind me. For a moment I wasn't sure what she wanted, then I understood: she was looking for my autoharp. 'Sing,' she said again, firmly.

'I don't have my instruments with me right now, Liza,' I said.

The group had stopped, and I realized that many eyes were surveying me expectantly. I was still wearing my gardening clothes, which were not exactly clean, and my hair was loosely tied in a ponytail which had mostly come undone. I could not have looked very respectable.

'I'm Shane,' I said to the sea of waiting faces. 'I met Liza, here, a little while ago.'

'Her name is Annie,' a tall, grey-haired man said, extending his hand to me. 'I'm Tristan Fowler, co-ordinator of the Drumlin Therapeutic Unit.' He looked to be in his early fifties, was athletically built, and spoke with a clipped English accent. He was dressed in denim shorts and a short-sleeved shirt, his silver hair cut in a tight military style.

'Good to meet you,' I said. 'I didn't mean to intrude, it's just that I've been wondering about this young lady ever since I ran into her.'

'I take it you taught her her new song,' Tristan said. Liza – or Annie, as I now knew she was called – was leaning against him, her arm wrapped about his broad shoulders.

'I did.'

'Are you a musician?'

'Yeah. I play some of the local pubs.'

'Well, we would love it if you would consider coming and doing a little concert for us, wouldn't we, lads?'

The group all whooped and cheered. One short, smiling youth with long blond hair slapped me on the back. I grinned and blushed sheepishly.

'Yeah, okay,' I said. 'I'm sure I can do that.'

Tristan fished a card out of his pocket. 'Here's my number. You'll get me there most mornings before ten. After that, we're into the programme, so it'll be hit and miss.'

'Thanks. I'll call you.'

Tristan nodded. 'I hope you do. Come on, lads.'

And off they went. I wandered back to the Austin, looking at the white card. Drumlin (Therapeutic) Training Unit it read. Co-ordinator: Tristan Fowler. Assistant Co-ordinator: Beth Singleton. Underneath were telephone and fax numbers, and an email address. In the corner of the card was the image of a standing stone. I stood by my car, and wondered why I felt so privileged to have been asked to do something for free during the day that I was paid well to do at night. Something told me that Tristan Fowler was an unusual man. My suspicion would prove to be true.

3

I worked hard for the next two days, and finished off the garden. I had promised Tristan Fowler I would play music for him and his clients, but now that a little distance had been put between us, and knowing that Annie was in a safe place on at least an occasional basis, I was more or less happy to forget the whole affair, and get back to my leisurely pace of life.

One evening, a week or so later, I was sitting in an old chair outside my front door, an old Spanish guitar slung across my knee and a bottle of beer on the windowsill beside my ear. I had fallen in love with an old American mountain song called 'When First Unto This Country', and I was trying to work out my own version of it. So far, searches of my record collection had unearthed several interpretations, none of which I felt quite suited me.

This has always been my method: I need to wear a song in before I'm happy to perform it in front of an audience. This can mean trying it out on several instruments, in a variety of tempos and in perhaps two or three different keys, until I've found what I tend to think of as a comfortable fit. It can take me anything from a week to a month, and is a constant part of my life. As the process unfolds, I develop a sense of the song; who the protagonists are; what the overall atmosphere and emotion is; not to mention developing a feel for the imagery and structure. I've always got one or more song on the go, and can be running over verses or considering possible chord sequences while I'm driving or cooking.

I was enjoying the early evening warmth, and was close to finding my own take on the song. The Spanish guitar I was plucking was the instrument I had first learned to play on, so it almost felt like an extension of myself. My mother had bought it for herself when I was a child. She took guitar lessons for a while, but the demands of teaching in a school for children with learning difficulties and being a mother to three growing children had finally distracted her from her musical studies. The guitar gathered dust in our living room for several years, until one wet afternoon I took it up out of boredom and began to slowly pick out the chords to 'House of the Rising Sun'.

I was singing softly, and picking out the jaunty riff I had developed, when my reveries were interrupted by the jangling of my phone, which was sitting on the kitchen table. I caught it just before it went to voicemail.

'Mr Dunphy?'

'Speaking.'

'My name is Tristan Fowler. We spoke some time ago about your coming in to play some music for me.'

'Um . . . yeah. I remember.'

'Did you lose my card?'

I considered letting him think so, then decided to be honest.

'No. I just assumed you were being polite when you asked me. And, if I'm truthful, I never bothered to follow up on it.'

'I see. Well, Annie is waiting very patiently for your visit. Music means a great deal to her, you see. Now, you might think she is a sweet simpleton who would not be able to recall someone new for more than a day or so, but please let me assure you that is genuinely not the case.'

'I didn't think that,' I said. 'I just got busy with other things and let it slip from my mind. I'm sorry.'

'Well, when shall we see you, then?'

'How did you get this number, Mr Fowler?'

'You told me you play in the local pubs. I assumed your most local would be the one closest to where we met. I told them I was looking for your services, and they happily passed on your contact details.'

'Resourceful,' I said.

'Thank you. Are you busy tomorrow morning?'

'No.'

'How would half past ten suit you, then?'

'Where are you based?'

He gave me directions, which I scribbled on the back of an envelope.

'Okay. I'll see you tomorrow morning.'

'I'm counting on your being there,' Tristan said. 'I'll be telling my group first thing that you're coming.'

'I'll be there.'

'I shall look forward to it.'

I hung up, shaking my head. My bluff had been well and truly called.

4

Drumlin (Therapeutic) Training Unit was based in a small one-storey building that had once been a grain store, situated half a mile from a small town not far from where I lived. Tristan Fowler met me at the door, and brought me into a small office, the walls of which were covered with photographs of him and many individuals who were obviously his clients. Some of the photos had been taken at a variety of events with local politicians and celebrities.

'Just to briefly explain to you what we're about here, Shane,' Tristan said when we were both seated. 'Drumlin is a unit I established more than ten years ago now, especially for young people with mild mental handicaps.'

'I didn't think that term was used any more,' I said.

Tristan raised an eyebrow. 'It's not. I was using language I thought you'd understand.'

'You don't need to go easy on me,' I said. 'I think I can keep up.'

'Fair enough. I noticed when I came here from the UK that there was a tendency to place individuals from right across the disability spectrum together, regardless of ability. So people who were actually only borderline, who were, in fact, pretty much able to do most things independently, but perhaps required a little support in one area, were placed in units alongside service users who were profoundly disabled.'

I nodded. 'Which didn't do either of them any good.'

'Exactly. What I saw happening was that those who were of a higher functioning either shot ahead of their less able colleagues, leaving them to languish, or all the attention was lavished on those of lower capacity, and the brighter lads and lasses would become angry and frustrated. Both scenarios led to terrible problems – violent outbursts, group conflict, or at the other end of the scale depression and withdrawal.'

'So you sought funding to set this place up?'

Tristan smiled. 'Not exactly. I came to Ireland with my wife, Heddie, who is involved in the financial sector. I'm a social worker by profession, but I have a second degree in applied psychology, which I got when I was in the army. We built a house in Ballytober, just down the road from here, and I started doing some voluntary work a couple of days a week in a day-care centre that was attached to the church there.'

'Very generous of you.'

'Well, we had some land and initially I planned to do a little farming: raise some goats and some chickens, perhaps.'

'How'd that go? I've got similar plans myself.'

'Oh, it's a sideline. But this has sort of taken precedence.'

I grinned. 'Funny how that can happen.'

'When I saw how one of our lads, a young fella called Max, was doing really badly, I knew I had to do something. I mean, this kid was just full of anger and resentment.' Tristan stood up, and took a picture down from among the gallery on the wall. It was a shot of a much younger Tristan Fowler (his hair was a little longer, and shot through with deep, sooty black) with his arms around the shoulders of a handsome brawny boy with the distinct features of Down's Syndrome. 'That's Max. He was ruling the roost at home, and was holding the staff at the centre to ransom, too. Well, I took it on as a project to try and bring him round, but I soon began to see that in such an environment there was just no way to make any lasting changes. I'd guide him forward three steps but within a week we'd have gone back five. So I called together the parents of half a dozen of the kids I knew were the most in need of a specialist setting, and asked them if they'd come with me if I established just that.'

'And the rest is history,' I said.

'More or less. We operated for the first five years without any funding other than what we could scrimp from those parents who could afford it. A local factory gave us a room to work out of, and I begged one of the hotels to let us use their swimming pool. St Fiachra's school said we could use their gym once a week. I picked up some carpentry tools in a car-boot sale, and made workbenches and tables for our craft room. Staff were either volunteers, like my colleague, Beth, or were accessed through Community Employment Training schemes.'

'Which meant they weren't qualified,' I added.

'Last year the Health Services finally recognized what I do. We now get core funding, and the wages of my people are on a par with others at their level.'

'That's no small achievement,' I said. 'The downside, I'd guess, is that by paying you, the managers from Community Services think they can tell you what to do.'

'They do try.'

'I'll bet they've tried to palm a few clients your way, too.'

Tristan smiled ruefully. 'They have.'

'And I'll bet they were all outside the mild range you have insisted on.'

Tristan nodded. 'Virtually every one.'

'Taking state money is a little bit like selling your soul, sometimes,' I said.

The older man was looking at me with a curious expression. 'You look like a musician,' he said, slowly, 'and I hear that you can certainly play. But I'm getting the sense you might have some experience in my area of expertise, too.'

I waved away the comment. 'Ah, I've done a bit of this and a bit of that in my time,' I said. 'Am I going to play for ye, or has this been a wasted journey?'

'Not at all,' Tristan said. 'Follow me.'

He led me through a short hallway into a large activity room, and there, already seated in a tight circle, was the group. I spotted Annie beaming among them.

24

'This is Shane, everyone, and he's going to play some music for us,' Tristan said. 'Why don't you all introduce yourselves, so Shane doesn't feel like a stranger?'

While I unpacked my steel-stringed acoustic guitar and harmonicas, Tristan went about the circle of people. Some told me their names willingly, others had to be prompted to say anything, and still others, like Annie, would not say anything at all. With Tristan was a grey-haired attractive woman of about the same age, who told me she was Beth Singleton, the assistant co ordinator and medical officer for the unit. There were three other staff members: a girl in her mid-twenties, called Valerie Keating; a middle-aged man, who introduced himself simply as Baz and a matronly older woman named Millie Yardley. By the time everyone's name had been given (or at least all those who wished to part with the information), I was seated and ready to go.

'Okay,' I said. 'As you know, I'm Shane, and I know lots of songs, but before I begin, maybe you could tell me what kind of music you like to listen to. Would any of you like to let me know what your favourite song is, or the singer you enjoy the most?'

'Me, Beth,' a very well-built and handsome youngster said, looking at the woman, and then giggling and covering his face.

'What would you like to say, Dominic?' Beth asked, trying to peep behind the boy's hands. 'What would you like to tell Shane?'

'I tell 'im,' Dominic said.

'What would you like to tell him, Dominic?'

The young man giggled again. During this time he had not made eye contact with me, or anyone else. 'I tell him my favourite singer?'

'Okay, Dominic,' I said. 'I'd love to know who your favourite singer is.'

'I tell 'im, Beth?'

'Go on, Dominic. We're all waiting,' Beth said, gently.

Dominic raised his eyes to me, and I saw for the first time that, had he not had the eyes and posture of a nervous child, he would have been devastatingly handsome – beautiful, even. He had clear blue eyes, a porcelain complexion, straw-blond hair, and the physique of an athlete. He giggled nervously again, took a deep breath, and said, 'My favourite singer is Daniel O'Donnell.' The name of the well-known Irish easy-listening singer was uttered with deep pride.

'Yeah, I like Daniel O'Donnell too,' a tiny woman, who had told me her name was Ricki, agreed.

'Me too,' Max, the man Tristan had told me about, said.

I was getting that sinking feeling in the pit of my stomach I get when I know a performance is about to go down the tubes. I did not know one single song by Daniel O'Donnell.

'Okay,' I said. 'Well, seeing as you all like wee Daniel so much, I bet you can sing me some of his songs. Right?'

Max looked at me with some suspicion. 'You are s'posed to sing for us,' he said, dubiously.

'Ah, yes,' I retorted, 'but I will be looking for you to sing along, so I need to know how good you all are. That's reasonable, isn't it?'

'Yeah,' Ricki agreed. 'I think that's only fair.'

Before I had another word out of my mouth, Dominic, his eyes closed and his head on one side, was singing in a sweet, very tuneful voice:

'Stand beside me, stand beside me
For if I should lose you I just couldn't get anywhere . . .'

I found the key he was singing, and joined in on guitar. The rest of the gathering were singing along in no time, and I breathed a sigh of relief. My ruse had worked: the room was full of smiles and singing voices.

5

An hour later Tristan called a halt to the music. I had enjoyed myself thoroughly, and to my delight I soon discovered that there was a knowledge of much more than just the collected works of Daniel O'Donnell among my listeners. We touched on everything from the Beatles to Bruce Springsteen to Ella Fitzgerald, and ended on Woody Guthrie's 'This Land Is Your Land', which was sort of the anthem of the unit. Being a huge Woody Guthrie fan, I was extremely impressed by this news.

'Okay, lads,' Tristan said. 'Story time, next. Let's get ready.'

Everyone picked up the chairs they had been sitting on, and placed them back round a large table at the other end of the room. I followed suit, then began to put away my instruments.

'That was very enjoyable,' Tristan said to me.

'I'm glad.' I grinned. 'Once we got over the Daniel O'Donnell stumbling block, it seemed to take off well enough.'

'Ah, yes.' Tristan laughed. 'You handled that very well.'

'It's an old trick for dealing with requests I don't know. Listen, thanks for asking me. I'll get out of your hair.'

'Well, thanks for coming along.'

We were shaking hands when Ricki came over and whispered something in Tristan's ear. It was hard to put an age on her; she could have been anything from twenty to fifty. She was perhaps only half an inch over four feet in height, and wore glasses with almost impossibly thick lenses. On her head was a shock of dark black curls, which were starting to grey about the temples.

Tristan listened carefully. 'Well, perhaps you should ask him yourself, Ricki.'

The little woman nodded, and looked at me bashfully.

'We were wonderin' if you might like to stay for story time, and maybe then have a bit of lunch with us,' she said. 'Please.'

I had not been expecting this invitation, and for a moment I didn't know what to say. 'Well, that's very kind of you,' I said. I glanced over to a section of the big room where there were three bookshelves and an array of beanbags and stuffed chairs. The group were all gazing in my direction, awaiting an answer. I had enjoyed myself so far. I didn't have anything else to do that morning – my plans did not go any further than possibly going for a run, which I could do later. And I always loved stories. 'I'd be delighted to stay for a while.'

Ricki held out her hand for me to take. 'Come on, then. We've got lots of stories to get through, today.'

Tristan laughed. 'Well, that's telling you,' he said. 'I'll bring your stuff into the office. You'd better go on. Who's going first, Ricki?'

'Annie.'

'Very good. I'll join you in a moment.'

Beth led me over to the others. I noticed for the first time that the room was divided up into six different sections. The centre was taken up by a long dining table, and then a large empty space, where the chairs had been arranged for our singing. There was the small library and reading area, where everyone was then gathered; on the opposite wall was a long woodwork area, with plenty of tools and half-finished pieces of work; there was a space where easels were set up, and I could see shelves with paints, pastels and other art accessories upon them; and there was a corner where many different kinds of old clothes were hung up, obviously for drama and role play.

When we were all seated, the carer who was called Millie said: 'Now, Annie, you have a story for us today?'

Annie sat up very straight, and waited while all eyes fell on her. Finally, she said, 'Boy. Him walkin' out. Cryin'.'

'Why is he cryin', Annie?' someone asked.

Annie swallowed and took a deep breath. I could see that

this was not an easy process for her, and required a huge effort in terms of concentration and energy. 'Wants Daddy,' she said.

'My daddy dead,' Max said.

'My daddy pickin' me up at four o'clock,' Dominic said.

'Daddy gone,' Annie said. 'Him cryin'. Wants Daddy. Daddy gone.'

'Where is this little boy out walking, Annie?' Millie asked. 'Is he in a town?'

Annie shook her head. 'Trees. Sky. Stars. Wind. Cold.'

'He's out in woods – a forest, maybe?'

Annie nodded emphatically.

'And it's night time.'

More nodding.

'And he's all alone, and he wants his daddy?'

'Is he a small boy, like my brother?' a boy with alarmingly red hair said.

Annie shook her head.

'Is he a little boy, or a big boy?' Valerie, the other staff member asked.

Annie held her hand high above her head.

'He's a big boy, then,' Beth said.

'Dominic,' Annie said.

'Big like Dominic,' Valerie said.

'No, *Dominic*,' Annie said, firmly.

'I. Am. Dom – in – *ic*!' Dominic said.

'Yes, he's like Dominic,' Valerie said, trying to work out what Annie was trying to tell her.

'No,' Annie said, the exasperation telling in her voice. '*Him* Dominic.'

There was a chorus of oohs and ahhs from everyone.

'So the lost boy *is* Dominic,' Beth said.

'Her talkin' 'bout me,' Dominic said, giggling heartily.

'So why is he out at night, all alone, crying for his daddy?' Valerie asked. 'Dominic's daddy would never let anything bad like that happen, would he?'

'No one there,' Annie said, quietly. 'Dark. Cold. All alone.'

I listened, particularly moved by the tone of Annie's voice: she was saying these words as if she knew exactly, from close personal experience, what they meant.

'I don't think I like this story,' Max said.

'Well, do you have a story for us, then?' Tristan said. He had just come back into the room, and pulled over a beanbag to join the group.

'Yeah,' Max said. 'Yeah, I do.'

'What's your story about then?'

Max beamed all over his face, quite obviously delighted to be the centre of attention. 'My story is about a giant robot,' he said.

'That sounds like an interesting story, all right,' Tristan said.

I found that I was only half listening to Max, though. My attention was still very much on Annie, and the haunting image she had painted in her simple yet dark story. While Max described his metal monstrosity, the girl sat, her lips still moving as she continued to recount her story to herself. I could not help but wonder how it ended.

More than a year would pass before I found out.

6

Over lunch, Tristan told me a little about some of the clients who made up his little group.

'Max and Annie you know about,' he said. 'Dominic was something of a conversation piece this morning, which is unusual, as he's fairly quiet these days, but let me assure you, he didn't used to be.'

While we talked, Beth Singleton cut bread and buttered it, diced up an avocado, laid out some freshly cut smoked ham and poured coffee. I was more than a little embarrassed to be waited on in such a manner, but Tristan seemed to accept it as the norm. Everyone else about the table had their own packed lunches, and got on with the business of eating, chatting and joking enthusiastically.

'No? He seems a very gentle good-natured sort of chap,' I said.

'You should have seen him three years ago. He was almost unmanageable.'

'What's his . . . um . . . condition?' I asked.

'His what?'

'Why is he intellectually disabled?'

'Oh, my apologies. Yes, well it's brain damage, you see. Our Dominic has quite severe epilepsy. It's under control now, but it took the medics a long time to get the drugs properly balanced to keep the seizures at bay. When that young man was six, he had a grand mal seizure which lasted for almost half an hour. The strain of it scrambled his mental functioning. He never properly recovered.'

Epilepsy is a fairly common neurological disorder characterized by recurring unprovoked seizures, which are caused by irregular neuronal activity. In other words, the epileptic experiences surges of electricity along the wiring in the brain, which either bring on convulsions or alternatively cause the system to shut down completely. Seizures are generally broken down into *petit* and *grand mal* (directly translated this means 'little' and 'big sickness'). Petit mal seizures are short, and simply take the form of the individual passing out for a few moments. Grand mal seizures involve passing out as well, but also the rapid tensing and relaxing of the muscles, which creates the stereotypical shaking and trembling that most people associate with epilepsy. Such seizures usually do not last for more than five minutes.

'Half an hour? He's lucky to be alive at all,' I said.

'If he gets them now, poor chap, they're generally very brief petits. When I met him first, though, he was still having grand mals, and he would get very sick with them. So here we had a young man – he was thirteen at that time – who could not understand why these things were happening, why he was feeling so wretched. He was a big bloke even then, and if anyone dared to say "no"' to him, he'd rear up with those fists of his and, let me tell you, you'd want to get out of the way fairly fast. He had his mum and dad terrorized, and no school would touch him.'

'That face couldn't have helped things. He looks like he was carved by Michelangelo.'

'Well, quite. He was so used to getting his own way, by hook or by crook, that he just believed the world owed him a living, and he would plough through anyone or anything that got in his way.'

'What did you do?' I asked, genuinely interested. I couldn't even begin to think how I would handle a challenge like that.

'I started saying no, and I meant it.'

'He didn't try to dissuade you?'

'I am not easily dissuaded. You have to remember, this was a young man who did not know how to stop the cycle of behaviour he was locked into. He would come in here, and within five minutes there would have been a blow-up, and he'd be lashing out, in tears ... I'm not a big believer in the time-out system, but there was nothing else to be done. Could you imagine him taking a swing at Ricki, there, or little Elaine?' He motioned at a small, dark-haired girl with Down's Syndrome who was sitting opposite me. 'We had to isolate him until he calmed down, which he hated.'

'And did he understand that he had to get himself under control before he rejoined you all?'

'Remarkably quickly. Don't misunderstand me, he fought it, but Dominic is a classic example of someone who *wanted* to be helped. He needed the control we placed on him, and the structure, and the guidance. He has thrived here. And let me assure you, he is a surprising person. There are depths to him that I'm still discovering. And by showing him how to be happy, we have saved a family. His parents were on the verge of having him institutionalized – they had no choice.'

'And Ricki?'

'Ricki *was* institutionalized for a long time. If you look at her file, she is classified as a "dullard", which is a term that has not been written on an official document for a very long time.'

'What age is she?'

'Almost fifty. Her mother had her outside wedlock, a big enough scandal at that time, but to have a child with a series of congenital abnormalities to boot – the family never took her home from the hospital.'

'So how did she end up here?'

'I came across Ricki in an institution. Her real name is Ricardo, after some daft saint or other. She had completely sunk into herself. She was miserable, uncommunicative, probably ready to die. I don't doubt that she would have done, if I'd left her there.'

'What, were you visiting on the look-out for clients or something?'

Tristan laughed.

'Dear me, no. Do you recall I told you that I volunteered in a centre attached to a church? Well, the priest who ran that setting was friends with one of the nuns who looked after Ricki. She told him how worried she was about this little creature who was pining away in her asylum. The priest asked me to see if I could help.'

I sipped some coffee.

'And does she still live there?'

'I arranged for her to be moved to a community house. It was one of the first things I did. As you saw today, Ricki was chosen by the group to invite you to join us. She is caring, sensitive, really quite bright in many ways. In the institution, she spent her days doing virtually nothing. She rarely spoke to anyone from one day to the next; she would sit about watching daytime television, drinking endless cups of tea ... is it any wonder she was about to give up the ghost?'

'And the nuns didn't mind you taking her away?'

'They weren't bad people, Shane. They were just ... misguided, I suppose.'

I nodded. 'I don't think I've ever been anywhere like this before.'

'Drumlin is a community,' Tristan said. 'Here there is no such thing as disability. There are no allowances made. I expect all our young people to strive to be the best they possibly can be, to take responsibility for their own actions and the consequences of them. If Drumlin is to work, we all have to believe in it. Have you noticed we all sit round the table and eat together? I've worked in places where the "disabled" trainees sat at one table, and the "staff"' – he made inverted commas in the air with his fingers – 'sat at another. That always struck me as a kind of apartheid. I won't have it here.'

'So I see.'

'I've had staff ask me when they get their lunch break. It can be a real stumbling block for some people. As far as I am concerned, the experience of eating together, sharing that essential human experience, is one of the most profound things anyone can do. Why would I want to deny anyone that?'

As we had been speaking, I noticed that each wall had a series of colourful pictures placed near the ceiling.

'What are those?' I asked.

'That, Shane, is our timetable. I think it's important that everyone here knows what's coming up and when. So craft is denoted by a hammer, or a pair of knitting needles. Story time by a book. Drama by the comedy/tragedy masks.'

'How do they know which day it is?'

'Do you see the green arrow over the door?'

'I do.'

'That's the beginning. So the first sequence of images is Monday, and so on.'

I nodded. 'Very clever.'

'Not really. But it works. Everyone can look up, at any time, and see what'll be happening in an hour's time, or in two days' time, for that matter. It adds a level of security.'

'So ten thirty on Wednesday, is that always music time?'

Tristan laughed. 'No. As you can see, we usually have art at that time. But then life can sometimes reach in and throw the best-made plans awry. Everyone here knows that we will sometimes step out of the programme. But I always give advance warning, and it's always something worth doing.'

'I see.'

'Who knows, maybe you'll come back, and we can make music a more regular fixture.'

I smiled at that, and said nothing. But it set me thinking.

PART 2

Terms and Conditions Apply

There was a naughty boy,
And a naughty boy was he,
He ran away to Scotland
The people for to see –
There he found
That the ground
Was as hard,
That a yard
Was as long,
That a song
Was as merry,
That a cherry
Was as red –
That lead
Was as weighty,
That fourscore
Was as eighty,
That a door
Was as wooden
As in England –
So he stood in his shoes
And he wonder'd,
He wonder'd,
He stood in his shoes
And he wonder'd.

From 'A Song About Myself'
by John Keats

7

Two weeks later, almost to the day, I returned from a morning jog to find Tristan Fowler parked outside my house in a ramshackle wood-panelled Citroën that was probably older than my Austin Allegro. He got out and waited as he saw me coming up the road.

'I hoped I'd catch you,' he said. 'I've got a proposition.'

'Come on in,' I said, opening the gate (it had been hanging off when I arrived, but I had fixed it and given it a fresh lick of paint) and standing back for him to go on up the short path.

Once inside, I brought my guest into the tiny living-room area of the cottage, and put the kettle on for coffee. I poured myself an orange juice, and then sat down opposite Tristan.

'What can I do for you?'

'You haven't exactly been honest with me, Shane,' Tristan said.

I shook my head. 'I don't follow.'

'Some of the things you said when you were at the centre struck me as odd, and I thought I might do a little checking up on you.'

'Why?' I asked.

'Oh, I just had a feeling about you,' Tristan said, enigmatically. 'Well, I had an interesting conversation with William, Annie's father. He told me you dropped her home, that evening you met her, and that you had Douglas Bellingham from the Ragged Fox pub in the car with you. Douglas, when I spoke to him, informed me that you had mentioned having done what he called "social welfare" work. When I dug a little deeper, I discovered that you've got quite a job history. Up until recently, you worked for Ben Tyrrell.'

'You know Ben?'

'I worked with him across the water.'

My old boss had worked extensively in the UK, and was something of a legend in social-care circles.

'Well, I admire your determination, I think,' I said. 'But what has any of this got to do with the price of beans? Yes, I worked with Ben. Yes, I have a bit of experience of social-care work. I didn't tell you because ... well, I suppose because I don't do that any more.'

'Why ever not?' Tristan asked, sounding genuinely puzzled. 'Ben tells me you have a real talent for it.'

'Well, Tristan, there are a few cases I could mention that would suggest otherwise.'

'Oh come on, Shane. That's just daft. There are always cases that don't work out; it's the nature of the job. You were working at the very sharp end of child protection for many years. If you hadn't lost now and again, I'd think you were being dishonest.'

'Yeah, well I don't think I want to have that sort of experience any more,' I said. 'I like it here. I like the peace and the quiet and the simplicity. I've thought about things a good deal since coming out here, and I believe very firmly that I made the best decision for everyone concerned when I left the Dunleavy Trust. I was totally burnt out, and I'm in no way convinced that I was thinking straight.'

'Yes, but that was almost a year ago, now.'

I shrugged.

'Sure. I've been recharging my batteries. But I'm not ready to go back. I deserve the break.'

I got up and made a pot of coffee. When I came back, Tristan was flipping through my CDs. 'You have eclectic tastes,' he said.

'A man for all seasons,' I said. 'So is that all you've come for? To tell me you've found me out?'

'No,' Tristan said. 'I would like you to come and work for me.'

I sighed deeply and poured us both some coffee. 'Have you not listened to a single word I said, Tristan?'

'I am not asking you to get involved with child protection. What we do at Drumlin is very different. The vast majority of our clients have been through their tough times and are reasonably happy and well adjusted. What we're about is bringing them to a place of independence, or as much as they can cope with.'

'I appreciate the offer, Tristan, I really do, but I am just not interested,' I said as firmly as I could without raising my voice. 'I've got other things to focus on now. For instance, I need to spend some time thinking about what I really want to do with the rest of my life, and what motivations have driven me to make the choices I've made up to this point.'

'So you're going through a selfish phase?' Tristan said.

'You could say that,' I returned, more than a little offended (probably because he was perfectly correct), 'but then Ben Tyrrell always told me that care workers must use their capacity to form relationships as the main tool of their trade. That means you are required to look after your emotional well-being – keep it serviced and maintained just like any piece of equipment you'd use for any other job. At the moment, my emotional well-being is in for a service.'

'Touché,' Tristan said, bowing ever so slightly.

'Look, I'm genuinely flattered,' I said, more gently, 'but you've got to understand, I just don't have any hunger for the job any more. Playing music suits me. I'm my own boss, there's no real demands placed on me, beyond being asked to play "The Fields of Athenry" every night, which I can just about cope with – this semi-retirement is for the best. You'll have to trust me on that.'

'And yet when you came across Annie Kelleher, you were

drawn to her immediately,' Tristan said. 'You interceded with those who would have hurt her, you took her from harm's way and brought her home.'

'Anyone else in my place would have done the same thing.'

'Would they? Douglas told me he would have left her on the street.'

'He didn't, though. He let me bring her into the pub, and went with me up the mountain.'

'Those men on the street intended to beat her, or worse.'

'Idle bravado . . . Tristan, this is going nowhere. Thanks, but no thanks.'

Tristan nodded sadly. 'You will come and play for us again? Stop in from time to time for lunch?'

'I would be delighted to.'

'The lads speak of you often. You were quite the hit with them all.'

'Flattery will get you nowhere, Mr Fowler,' I said, standing and opening the living room door for him.

'I wouldn't be here if their reaction hadn't told me strongly that you were the right man for the job.'

I watched him drive off in his antique car, and felt a strange emptiness. There was a part of me that wanted what he was offering. I had felt completely at home at Drumlin, and knew that I could slot into the day-to-day running of the place with ease. But I also knew that I would be being unfair to myself and the pledge I had made if I did. I went back inside and stood under the hot spray of the shower for a long time.

8

Sometimes I think that the universe plays tricks on me.

Halfway through the gig that night, as I was playing 'This Land Is Your Land', the door of the pub opened, and in walked Ricki.

She was with two others whom I guessed came from her community home, and they sat right under the small stage and sang and clapped and enjoyed themselves greatly. When the time came for my break, I got a drink and sat down with them.

Ricki introduced me to her friends, blushing dreadfully.

'Now Ricki, I've been playing here every Tuesday night for the past two months, and I've never seen you,' I said. 'What brings you along tonight?'

'Every month, we go somewhere different for a few drinks,' my new friend said. 'We likes a bit of music, and Frank, who runs our house, tells us it's good for us to look in the papers to see who's playin' about the county, and then organize to get there.'

'Book a taxi or whatever,' one of her friends, Ross, a plump, moon-faced man, said.

'So, we was checkin' the ads in the local paper,' Ricki continued, 'and I seen your name, and at first I wasn't sure if it was you or not, but then I asked Tristan, and he said it was, so I asked Ross and Terrence if we might like to come and see you tonight.'

'Well, I'm very glad you did,' I said.

'Yeah, we're glad we came,' said Terrence, a tall thin kid who looked to be no more than sixteen, and was drinking a glass of orange. 'You play some very good music.'

'Thank you, Terrence,' I said.

'Yeah, Terrence likes music,' Ricki said.

The group lapsed into silence. I watched them from the corner of my eye. Here they sat, in a crowded pub, engaged in an activity that was so simple, yet encompassed so many challenges for them. To choose a destination, to set up transport, to decide what to drink and where to sit, and to do all this without the safety net of a carer, must have been hugely frightening for this little family who spent most of their lives being told what to do, how and when to do it. I found myself suddenly filled with pride and admiration for them.

'Do you like going to Drumlin, Ricki?' I asked.

She looked up at me, blinking, considering the question seriously.

'I do, Shane. I like it very much.'

'Why?'

She took a swallow of her drink – a non-alcoholic beer – and scratched her head. 'Tristan and Beth have been very good to me,' she said at last. 'I used to live in a bad place, and Tristan came and took me from there, and gave me somewhere where they looked after me good.'

'The community home, where you are now?'

'Yeah. We looks out for each other there.'

'We're friends,' Terrence said.

'Best buds,' Ross said.

'I'm glad you like it,' I said. 'But why is Drumlin such a cool place to work?'

Ricki's brow furrowed and she shifted in her seat. ''Cause we do fun stuff, and that . . .'

'And you didn't do fun stuff in the last place?'

Ricki shook her head so hard I thought it might topple off. 'No. No way. In the institution, we didn't do nothin'. Every day was just the same as every other day. No one talked to you, no one asked if you were all right, no one laughed or smiled or cried or sang. All we ever done was pray. I didn't used to feel

44

like prayin' much, 'cause I didn't think I had a lot to say thanks to God for. Used to get in trouble for not sayin' me prayers.'

'So Drumlin is better than that?'

'Of course it is!' Ricki said, laughing at the suggestion that it might not be. 'Now, there are things we *have* to do, all right, but I know that even the things I don't like are there 'cause I need 'em. I finds readin' hard, 'cause I never really been to school much, but I'm gettin' lots and lots better. I can read most of what's in the paper, now. In the institution, I used to feel like I wasn't worth much. I thought I was there 'cause I was a bad sort of person. I thinked that I had to be to be locked in a place like that 'cause I done somethin' wrong. I used try really hard to remember what it was I done to deserve to be there, but I never could. But when I goes into Drumlin, I knows everyone is happy to see me and I'm glad to see them. When I says somethin', people listen. Tristan asks me what I think about things, and when he asks, he *really* wants to know. Them nuns, they never hit me or did bad things . . . they just did . . . nothin'.'

'So being in Drumlin has made your life better,' I said.

'Yes,' Ricki said simply. 'I would never, ever want to go back to the way things was before.'

We talked some more, about other, lighter things, but what she had said about Tristan, and the work being done in Drumlin returned to me later, as I drove home along the dark, tree lined country roads. Maybe, I thought, maybe it would be worth getting involved with these people. The question was: to what degree?

9

'Speak.'

'Devereux, it's Shane.'

Karl Devereux is a colleague of mine who works on a voluntary basis as a youth worker in the city. He grew up in a slum area, and served time in prison as a result of many years spent involved in organized crime. While some involved in social care find him difficult to deal with – and a little frightening – the many young people he helps every day see only a man who knows exactly what they are going through, and who wants to extend a hand of friendship. I had, over the years, found his advice and assistance invaluable.

'It's late. Call tomorrow.'

I looked at the clock over the fireplace. It was one thirty in the morning.

'It is tomorrow, Karl. Anyway, you weren't asleep.'

'And you know this how?'

'You don't sound as if you've just woken up.'

'And how would you know what I sound like when I've just woken up?'

I had no answer for that. 'Look, I need to run something by you.'

'Go on.'

'You work as a volunteer.'

'Yes.'

'Even though you've been offered paid work countless times.'

'Yes.'

'Why?'

'I want to retain my independence. My freedom. If I choose

to work on a case, or to help a particular child or family, then I do. If I prefer not to work with a group or an individual, then I don't. I make my own hours, come and go as I please, and am answerable to nobody.'

I considered this. 'And do you feel you're given access to all the information and support you need?'

'I have my own methods for accessing information and support.'

I had sometimes had need to use some of Devereux's sources in the past.

'Do you get the same respect as the paid staff for what you do?'

'From those who count.'

'But not from everyone?'

'I don't know any worker who is respected universally. My clients appreciate what I do. I know when I go to bed at night – when I'm not disturbed by ridiculous phone calls, that is – that I have done the best I can within parameters I believe in. How many people can say that?'

'Fair enough, Karl. Sorry to have bothered you.'

'How are things out in the sticks?'

'Good so far.'

'I was never a fan of country living. All that clear air tends to clog up my lungs.'

'You'll have to come out and visit.'

'I'll consider it.'

'G'night, Karl.'

'Look after yourself.'

I hung up and poured myself a drink. A plan was beginning to form in my head, a way that I could get involved in what was happening in Drumlin, and still keep that little bit of distance I needed. I just hoped Tristan would go for it.

'You want to volunteer?' Tristan asked me for the second time.

'I do.'

'Work for me for no wage?'

'Yes.'

'But I just offered you a job – a paid job – and you turned me down. Now you arrive in my office, and ask me if you can come and work here for nothing. Pardon me if I'm a bit confused.'

I sat forward and leant my elbows on Tristan's desk. 'I don't want to get caught up in contracts and conditions of employment and dental plans and all that stuff. I want to be able to come in here a couple of days a week, help out, get involved in the programme, get a feel for what you do, and be free to go home at the end of the day without all the stuff I'd have buzzing around in my head if I were a member of staff.'

'You want the nice stuff without the responsibility, you mean,' Tristan said.

'I suppose you could put it that way.'

'I just did.'

Neither of us said anything.

'Well?' I prompted. 'What do you say?'

'I don't know. Even though you're not asking for any money, why do I feel as if you're pulling a fast one on me?'

'Maybe because you have an overly suspicious nature?' I suggested.

Tristan shook his head. 'There'd have to be some limits placed on it,' he said at last. 'You could do that music module I suggested.'

'I'd be happy to do that, but I'd want to do other things, too.

48

Look, you've come a long way towards winning me over. I want to get a taste of what Drumlin is all about. I want to see why you've managed to change the lives of the people who come here. Maybe I want a part of that healing, too.'

'Physician, heal thyself?'

'Maybe I think I can't sort my personal crap out on my own. Which is why I want to come here.'

'It's not all fun and games, Shane,' Tristan said. 'There's a tough side to Drumlin, too. Part of what you say you want to run away from is here. The world doesn't stop at the door.'

'I'm not completely naive,' I said. 'I know that, and I accept it. I'm not talking about coming here every day, or even every other day, from nine until five. But I would like to give it a go, and see what I make of it. Think of it like this: if we do it my way, you get me at no cost, and if I can't hack it and head for the hills, you've lost nothing.'

'Well, that's true.'

'This is the fairest, most honest way of doing business with you that I could find.'

Tristan nodded, and extended his hand across the table. 'Okay, let's give it a go. When do you want to start?'

'How about next Monday?'

'Next Monday it is.'

And that was how I came to Drumlin (Therapeutic) Training Unit.

PART 3

False Starts and Broken Hearts

When all the world is old, lad,
And all the trees are brown;
When all the sport is stale, lad,
And all the wheels run down;
Creep home, and take your place there,
The spent and maimed among:
God grant you find one face there,
You loved when all was young.

From 'Young and Old' by
Charles Kingsley

11

Drumlin's day usually began with what was referred to as 'news' but was in fact more a loose chat, in which the group brought one another up to date with what was going on in their lives. The chairs were set in a circle, everyone brought their cups of tea or coffee with them (I soon discovered that tea and coffee were viewed as being vitally important at Drumlin), and Tristan or Beth would kick off proceedings with whatever titbit of information they felt like sharing. It didn't seem to matter how apparently trivial such disclosures were (anything from a new pair of shoes to what was happening on *Eastenders* was discussed), what mattered was that everyone shared something. As Millie put it to me as we sat down: 'It's about making sure all our lads feel they have a voice and a safe place to air it. Don't think this is all just an excuse to talk shite for half an hour. Lots of fairly important stuff gets an airing here.'

Of course, it being my first day, I was destined to be the first item of news. Tristan called for hush, and opened proceedings.

'I'd like to welcome Shane Dunphy to the unit. You all know him from when he came here to sing and play for us, but he has asked me if we would mind him being in the group a few days a week. Now, I said I didn't mind, but this isn't my group. How do you all feel about it?'

That blind-sided me. I was under the impression I was in. Now, it seemed, I had another set of hurdles to get over.

'I like Shane,' Ricki said. I couldn't help but feel a swell of warm feelings for her. 'I think he would be good for our group.'

'Me talk,' Max said.

'Okay, Max,' Tristan said. 'Please tell us what you think.'

Max rubbed his knees, and surveyed me with a very serious expression. 'I want to welcome Shane to the group,' he said. He had a slightly halting manner of speaking, and the slurring that often accompanies Down's Syndrome. 'I think he will be a good man to have with us.'

Tristan repeated what Max was saying, to ensure I could understand him.

'And to start,' Max continued, 'he can make some more tea.'

A huge grin spreading across his face, Max made a drama of showing everyone his empty cup. The group, of course, thought this a fine joke, and there were calls from all sides for more tea.

'What about you, Dominic?' Beth asked. She was seated in her perennial position beside Tristan. 'Would you like to welcome Shane to Drumlin, or do you think we have enough in the group?'

Dominic smiled and formed his words carefully. 'I like Shane,' he said. Then, happy with this statement, almost as if he liked the sound of it: 'I like Shane!'

'Well that's another vote of confidence,' Tristan said.

Annie, when it came to her turn, said not a word, but walked over and threw her arms about my neck. 'Sweet boy,' she said into my ear, quietly. 'Nice man.'

I was beginning to think this was all just a formality, when the first voice of dissent was raised. Elaine, a pretty girl with Down's Syndrome, simply shrugged when asked about my joining the group. 'I don't know,' she said. 'I don't know him.'

'Well, I think that's fair comment,' Tristan said. 'I have a suggestion: why don't you ask Shane some questions about himself. You'll answer truthfully, won't you, Shane?'

I looked at Tristan, aghast. A public interview had certainly not been part of my plans for the day. 'Within reason,' I said.

'There you go, Elaine,' Valerie said. 'Here's your chance to get to know Shane better.'

'All right,' Elaine said. 'Why he want to come here?'

'Ask him,' Valerie said.

Elaine levelled her gaze in my direction. She was short and plump, and dressed in a plaid skirt, a pink blouse and light blue cardigan. Her hair was cut in that unfortunate bowl style many parents of children with Down's Syndrome seem to feel is attractive.

'Well?' Elaine said.

'I think what you do here is quite special,' I said. 'I want to learn more about it.'

'What you mean "what we do here"?' Elaine shot back.

'I'm impressed by watching you all work together. How you show one another respect. The way everyone has a part to play that is important. No one is seen as less or in any way . . . I don't know . . .'

'Handicapped?' Elaine said tersely. 'You wanna work wit the handicapped? Do it make you feel good?'

Max stood up like a shot at that comment.

'Me not handicapped!' he said. 'Elaine, no like that word!'

'In the group everyone has a right to speak their mind,' Tristan said. 'You've hurt Max's feelings, though, Elaine. I think you need to acknowledge how you've made him feel.'

'Sorry, Max,' the girl said, much more gently. 'I not sayin' you handicapped. Maybe it's what *he* think, though.'

All heads were turned in my direction. Inwardly cursing for letting myself be led into an ambush, I forced a smile onto my face. 'Elaine, I don't like that word either. I would never, ever call anyone here "handicapped". I know that can make people feel bad about themselves, and that's never right. But let me answer your question with a question of my own: does coming here make *you* feel good about yourself?'

Elaine didn't have to think about that. 'Yeah. So?'

'Well, I think you all know that I'm not from around this part of the country. I moved here from the city a little while ago. I suppose I was running away from some bad things that had happened to me.'

'What kind of things?' Joan, a girl who suffered from a very mild form of autism, asked.

I weighed this question for a moment. How honest should I be?

'I used to work with kids who were in trouble.'

'Trouble with the police?' Ricki asked.

'Yes, some of them. But some had parents who were mean to them, and some had no parents at all and had to live in institutions, like you did, Ricki, and some had been hurt by people –'

'Hurted how?' Elaine wanted to know.

'Some of them had been beaten a lot, and some had been . . . um . . . touched in a bad way.'

'Him's talkin' about sex now,' Elaine said matter-of-factly. 'Them kids was *sexually 'bused*.'

'Oh, that's a bad thing to happen to anyone,' Ricki said. 'I knew a girl when I was livin' with the nuns, and that happened to her in one place she stayed, and she wasn't never right after that.'

'My daddy's pickin' me up at four o'clock,' Dominic said very solemnly.

'And you helped these kids?' Elaine said.

'I tried to, yes. But sometimes, I wasn't able to.'

'Why?'

'All sorts of reasons. Sometimes they'd just been hurt too much. It didn't matter how much me and my friends tried to make them feel better, they'd seen too much pain and they couldn't hear what we had to say any more. Sometimes they were just too scared, and didn't believe we were going to help. They thought we were just waiting for a chance to hurt them, too. And then there were times when I didn't know what to do. I tried everything I could think of, and none of it worked.'

'So you stopped doin' that job?' Ricki said.

'Yes. It got so I didn't think I was much good at it any more. So I came here, and I started to play music for a living, and then I met all of you and you were nice and friendly, and you invited me to lunch. And I got to thinking that it might be pleasant to come to a place where people have smiles on their faces when they come in to work in the morning.'

The room went quiet. Glen, the boy with bright red hair, broke the silence. 'I didn't have a smile coming in here this morning,' he said. 'I most surely did not.'

'And why is that, Glen?' Beth asked.

'I wanted to stay at home and watch television. *The Love Boat* is being shown on UK TV Gold, and I would much prefer to be at home enjoying that show. Did you know they made a follow-up with the actor Robert Urich in the role of the captain?'

'I did not know that,' Beth admitted. 'But, Glen, we were discussing whether or not you'd like Shane to join the group.'

'Can you sing the theme song for *The Love Boat*?' Glen asked.

'I suppose I could,' I said, bewildered.

'I can sing it,' Glen said. 'If there are any lyrics you're unsure of, come and talk to me.'

'Okay, thanks. I will.'

'Did you ever see *The A-Team*?' Ricki asked Glen.

'I did. Did you know the actor Mr T, who plays the character of B. A. Baracus in *The A-Team*, plays the baddie in the film *Rocky III*?'

'Did he?' Ricki asked, fascinated.

'He did. That character is called Clubber Lang. He actually kills Rocky's trainer, Mickey, who is played by the great actor Burgess Meredith, who is best known for his role as the Penguin in the Batman series . . .'

And I was forgotten. I had, it seemed, passed the interview.

When Tristan finally declared that the group was closed, and we were to clear up for craft, I felt myself relax. I had not realized quite how tense I had been during the discussion, but as we put the chairs away, it occurred to me, like clouds parting and the sun coming out, that I wanted powerfully to become a part of this place and these people.

Lost in my thoughts for a few moments, I had not noticed Annie drifting over to me.

'Nice singing man,' she said, leaning over and kissing me on the check. 'Prickly face, he's got.'

'Hi, Annie,' I said. 'Thanks for helping me, just now.'

'L'il Liza Jane,' she said, making a motion in the air as if she were strumming the autoharp.

'That's right,' I said. 'That's our song, isn't it?'

She reached over and took my hand. Very gently, she opened my fingers, and placed something in the palm of my hand.

'What's this, Annie?' I asked.

'Present for you,' she said. 'Piece of my home. Piece of my heart.'

And singing in that haunting, off-key way she had, she half walked, half danced away. I looked at what she had given me. It was a highly polished piece of dark black stone – obsidian or onyx, maybe. It was almost perfectly round, and I wondered if she had found it, or bought it somewhere – in one of those angel shops that sells crystals, perhaps. It would be some time before I found out where my stone had come from – even though Annie, in her way, had already told me.

12

For the rest of the morning, Max followed me around like a puppy-dog. Every time I turned, there he was, beaming at me. When we did craft, he stood at my elbow, watching every movement I made. When we moved on to do some role-plays, he wanted to be in every single sketch I was asked to do. When Tristan asked me to pop into town to get some groceries for lunch, Max insisted on joining me, and strode about the supermarket, ceremoniously placing each item into the basket and consulting with me on prices and the quality of various brands.

I was secretly delighted. I had barely been in the unit a day, and I had bonded powerfully with a client who was obviously one of the more vibrant personalities in the place. When we sat down to eat, he was at my side, and matched me mouthful for mouthful.

'You seem to have made a friend,' Tristan observed.

'Looks like it,' I agreed.

'Just beware,' the older man said quietly, 'you can fall from favour as quickly as you rise to it. Don't get too complacent.'

'I'll keep it in mind,' I said, convinced Max and I were, by now, friends for life.

There was another new member – or at least occasional visitor – to the group that lunchtime. Tristan's wife, Heddie, came for a visit. She was a tall, avuncular woman, who spoke in a loud, booming voice with a slight Northern Irish inflection. It was impossible not to notice that while Heddie was about, Beth Singleton not only did not sit next to Tristan, but moved right over to the other side of the table. Heddie took her place in preparing Tristan's meal and serving him.

My nosiness got the better of me, and I could not resist asking Millie about it when we did the washing-up.

'Yes, it's a very strange arrangement,' she said. Max was off with the rest of the group, who had gone on a nature walk, so we could speak freely. 'The history of Tristan–Heddie–Beth is majorly bizarre.'

'How so?'

'Well, when Tristan came to Ireland initially, and was volunteering in St Sebastian's centre – do you know who the manager of that centre was?'

'Not Beth?'

'It was. *She* was managing *him*. Well, the word is that, before much time had elapsed, he was pretty much running the operation, and she was "Yes, Tristan" and "No, Tristan", just as you see her now. She was manager in name, but he was calling all the shots.'

'He does seem to know what he's about, in fairness,' I said.

'Oh, for sure. He's brilliant with the lads. No one, and I mean *no one*, can get any good out of Max Harrison except for Tristan. All of them love him. But the down side is that he can be a right bollix to work for at times. He'll sit and do all that group stuff: "Giving the young people a voice" and whatnot, and he genuinely cares about what they have to say, but the same can't always be said for us staff. Ninety-nine times out of a hundred, it's his way or no way at all.'

'He's a strong character, and that's a fact,' I said.

'It is widely accepted,' Millie went on, 'but mark my words, never said in either of their presences, that Tristan and Beth were at it like rabbits from very soon after he started working with her. It is also a generally held belief that Heddie Fowler worked out what was going on – and you'd have to be a complete imbecile not to be able to read the body language between them – and warned Beth that if she continued carrying on with her husband, she would fucking swing for her.'

'Ah, the poetry of the woman scorned.' I grinned.

'Indeed. But it doesn't end there,' Millie said.

'No?'

'Nope. See, Beth still virtually lives with the pair of them. She and Tristan regularly head off to fund-raising events together, and have little cosy dinners and such after work. You've seen the way she lays out his meals and almost spoon-feeds him at lunch. It's all very odd.'

'Well, maybe she's old-fashioned,' I mused. 'You know the way some people are.'

'What a lot of us think is going on is a long way from old-fashioned,' Millie said conspiratorially.

'Oh,' I said, 'do tell.'

'It has been proposed among certain factions that there is something of a *ménage à trois* in operation,' my companion almost whispered.

'Yeah, but wouldn't that sort of negate what you said earlier about Heddie swinging for Beth if she continued with her illicit intentions?' I said.

Millie nodded, sighing. 'It does — but the whole threesome thing is so much more fun, don't you think?

When the washing-up was finished, Millie and I laid out pens, paper and workbooks for remedial mathematics. Ten minutes later, everyone was back from their walk, and several little groups gathered about the room, working on various real-world numerical problems: if you bought a packet that had six crispie buns in it, and four of your friends came over, how would you make sure everyone got the same amount of cake, for example. While this was happening, I noticed Tristan at one of the workbenches, fiddling with an old stereo.

'Anything I can help with?' I asked, thinking I might continue my streak of success in DIY.

'I've had this machine for years,' Tristan said, a pair of bifocals balanced on the end of his long nose. 'We used to play some old vinyl records on it or have the radio on during craft and modules like that when it wouldn't be too much of a distraction. Last week, though, it packed up, and I'm buggered if I can get it working again.'

'Give us a look,' I said. 'Is power getting through to it?'

'Shane, do me the credit of having first checked to see if the plug needed rewiring.'

Twenty minutes later we were still at it, and I was totally befuddled. I had an inkling that Tristan was too, but we were both too macho to admit it. When the remedial session was over, Beth brought us both some tea.

'Maybe if you step back from it for a few minutes, boys, the answer will come to you,' she said, and went back to the others. Tristan and I stood, mugs in hand, staring at the damaged stereo. Minutes passed. Nothing occurred to either of us.

Presently, Dominic wandered over, towering over us both.

'Radio broke, Tristan?' he asked.

'It is, Dominic.'

'Radio broke, Shane?'

'Dead as a dodo, Dom,' I concurred.

Pause.

'I look, Tristan?' Dominic asked.

Tristan drank some tea. 'If you'd like to,' he said.

The tall boy bent low over the stereo, and began to fiddle.

'He's going to make things even worse,' I said out of the corner of my mouth.

'As you just said, the bloody thing's completely dead,' Tristan said. 'How can it get any more broken?'

Seconds later, Dominic stood back.

'You stick in the plug,' he said to Tristan.

'Okay,' the older man said. 'But we'd better put the back on first, just to be safe.'

Without even looking, Dominic picked up the plastic back of the machine, and clipped it on.

'Plug in now,' he said.

Tristan did as Dominic said. I pressed the 'on' switch, and to my huge surprise, static immediately began to emit from the speaker. In amazement, I adjusted the dial, found a station, and loud Top 40 music assailed our ears.

'Dominic,' I said, completely dumbfounded. 'What did you do?'

'I fixed it,' he said, and, giggling happily to himself, went back to where he had been sitting.

'I cannot fucking believe it,' I said, looking in wonderment at Tristan.

'One thing I've learned is to never underestimate our young people,' he said, shaking his head and smiling.

'Ain't that the truth,' I said.

Meg visited Drumlin three afternoons a week. She was probably in her late forties, had grey hair cut tight close to her head,
and wore shapeless, loose dresses that hung about her gaunt
figure like sackcloth. She had been attending Drumlin for a
year, when I first met her, and had thus far barely engaged with
the group at all.

'I don't know much about this one,' Tristan told me. It
was my second day at the unit. The rest of the group were
creating a huge map of the main street of the nearby town,
which they were constructing by making large images of each
of the buildings and sticking them on either side of a strip of
black card, which denoted the road. Meg would not participate, and was perched with her back to everyone, staring
at the wall. At least, I assumed she was staring at the wall;
when I looked a little closer, she seemed to have her eyes
closed.

'My understanding of her case is that she spent quite a few
years in a psychiatric hospital, but when cutbacks caused her
ward to be closed, she was farmed out to live with her uncle.
He doesn't seem to know what to do with her, so she is left to
her own devices while at home.'

'And wants to be left to her own devices here, too, by the
looks of things,' I said.

'Want to take a run at getting her to join us?' Tristan
suggested.

'She doesn't know me from Adam,' I pointed out.

'Maybe that'll work in your favour.'

'I'll give it a go. Don't expect much,' I said, and wandered
over to where Meg was sitting.

'Tristan asked me to come over and introduce myself,' I said. 'I'm Shane.'

'Meg,' the woman said, turning to show me her back.

'Pleased to meet you,' I said, not bothering to put my hand out to shake: she wouldn't have seen it, anyway. 'Meg, everyone's busy over there working on a really fun project. Wouldn't you like to join in?'

'No.'

'When it's done, we're going to put it up on the wall in the hallway on the way in to the unit so everyone can see it – visitors too.'

'Great.'

'You don't want to have a go?'

'No.'

I was tempted to give up then and there, but experience has taught me that luck favours the doggedly stubborn, and I figured that I might as well see if I could wear her down with tenacity.

'So you've been coming to Drumlin for a while, then?'
Silence.

'A year, is it? And what did you do before that?'
No response.

'At home with your uncle? Y'know, I have some uncles, but I never got to know them terribly well. They lived in England, mostly. I suppose that my family weren't really tight in that way. I wish I knew them better, though. I always kind of had a notion that an uncle might take me out fishing, or teach me how to carve wood, or something like that. Build a tree house. That kind of stuff. Does your uncle do cool things with you?'

Nothing.

'No? That must make you sad. Did you always live with him?'

Empty air.

'You were in a psychiatric hospital for a long time? What was that like?'

A slight tremor of the shoulders.

'Did you know that all the psychiatric hospitals in Ireland were built at the same time, all to the same design? They were built to last, you know, and the people who made them must have been very clever, because two hundred years later, they're all still standing, and most of them are still being used. Isn't that amazing?'

A greater tremor. A twitch, almost.

'Lots of them have farms attached to them. I visited one once that had its own reservoir. It was extraordinary, because all these eels had somehow gotten in – they can crawl overland, like snakes – and they'd gotten into this reservoir; they were top of the food chain and had grown to a pretty remarkable size. The nurses used to fish for them, and one of the patients knew how to make a smokehouse, and you could smell the smoked eel when you went outside. I'd never had eel before. It was quite nice.'

Slowly, by degrees, she was turning to look at me.

'I worked with some people who had to live in psychiatric hospitals for a while, and I'm going to be honest with you, I never really liked going to see them. They could be scary, lonely places. How long were you there?'

Quietly, so that I had to crane my neck to hear her she said, 'Thirty years.'

'That's a long time.'

''Tis.'

'Did you like it?'

'No.'

'Why were you there?'

'I had a baby.'

That stumped me.

'They put you into a hospital for the mentally ill because you had a baby?'

She nodded.

'That doesn't make sense, Meg. Were you very depressed, maybe, after you'd had the child?'

'No. The Magdalene, they had no bed for me.'

'Oh – oh God, Meg,' I said, as the penny dropped and I felt a sinking feeling in my stomach.

Magdalene Asylums were institutions for so-called 'fallen' women. They were initially meant for prostitutes, but as their popularity grew, they began to cater for those unfortunate females who became pregnant outside of wedlock, who were intellectually disabled, or who were simply too attractive for their own good and were in danger of garnering the attentions of the opposite sex.

Once a woman was interred in one of the asylums, she could not leave until a member of her family or a priest signed her out. These veritable prisons were operated by different orders of the Roman Catholic Church, most famously the Sisters of Mercy and the Good Shepherd Sisters. The inmates were required to undertake hard manual labour, most often laundry work, as a result of which in Ireland, such asylums became known as Magdalene Laundries. It has been estimated that 30,000 women were admitted during the 150-year history of these institutions, the vast majority against their will. Perhaps the most awful aspect of this horrendous part of Irish history is that, despite the fact that the police and the state colluded with the Church in what was, in actuality, a form of slavery, the incarceration of these poor women had no basis in law.

'So when the Magdalenes couldn't take you, your family had you committed?'

She nodded. 'I had my baby in the nuthouse, and they took him away from me, and I never seen him again.'

I reached out and took her hand. It sat limply in my own. I don't know if she was even aware of my touch, but I held her hand, anyway.

'What did you call him, Meg?'

Her face crumpled as tears came. 'I don't even know if my baby was a boy or a girl,' she said. 'They took him before I could see, and they told me I didn't need to know.'

She sobbed bitterly. I noticed peripherally that we were being watched from the other end of the room, but I ignored the eyes.

'What do you think your baby was? In your mind, when you think about it, do you see a boy or a girl?'

'A boy.'

'Okay. And what do you call him?'

'Robert.'

'That's a good name, Meg.'

She nodded, then put her head down on the table. I put my arm round her shoulders, and sat with her until she was quiet.

Meg didn't join the group that afternoon. We stayed where we were, away from the others, and she talked sporadically about her life. Robert's father had been a teacher of Meg's, a fact which had added to her family's shame at what had happened. During her time in the hospital, she had only been visited on a handful of occasions: to be informed of the death of a family member or when she needed medical treatment and forms had to be signed.

'I went mad in there,' she said. 'I was of sound mind when I went in, but you can't stay that way inside that place. I went mad. It was easier.'

When the bus came to bring the clients home, Meg stood up, squeezed my hand once, and followed the others out. I sat back, mentally and emotionally exhausted. Tristan came and pulled over a chair. 'You did good,' he said.

'Did I?'

'That cry has been coming for more than a year.'

'More than thirty years, maybe.'

'Tell me about it.'

I did.

'That teacher might not have retired,' I said. 'If he was just out of college, he could have ten years yet before he gets his gold watch.'

Tristan nodded. 'Did you get a name?'

'Mister Roberts.'

Tristan shook his head sadly. 'I'll look into it.'

I stood up. 'I'm going home.'

'You gigging tonight?'

'Yeah. Frankly, I could do with letting off some steam.'

'It's important to have a release valve.'

My performance that night was like a purge.

PART 4

Rough and Tumble

On the third day the messenger came back again, and said, 'I have not been able to find a single new name, but as I came to a high mountain at the end of the forest, where the fox and the hare bid each other good night, there I saw a little house, and before the house a fire was burning, and round about the fire quite a ridiculous little man was jumping. He had a hideous countenance, and a hump on his back, and his skin was like that of the oak tree. He hopped upon one leg, and shouted –

'To-day I bake, to-morrow brew,
the next I'll have the young queen's child.
Ha, glad am I that no one knew
that Rumpelstiltskin I am styled.'

From *Rumpelstiltskin* by
the Brothers Grimm

14

Beth was gazing into the fridge disconsolately. I noticed that, though the door was open, the light was not on, and the sour smell of turned milk was seeping into the kitchen.

'Problem?' I asked as I spooned coffee into one of the cafetières.

'I think it is obvious that the fridge is on the fritz,' Beth said testily.

'Nice alliteration,' I said.

She ignored my remark, and continued to stare into the bowels of the damaged appliance.

'We only got this a year ago. It should not have packed up already.'

'So call the store. It must be still under guarantee.'

Beth seemed to think that by staring at the rapidly decomposing foods in the refrigerator that a means to repair the mechanism might come to her.

'We didn't buy it in a store.'

'Well that was silly,' I said.

'As you well know, we operate on a shoestring. Almost everything here is second-hand.' She closed the door at last. 'I'd better see what Tristan thinks. He's handy with gadgets.'

Ten minutes later Tristan, Beth and several of the clients were standing gazing into the open fridge. My own DIY abilities, though developing rapidly, did not extend to any level of mechanical engineering, so I stayed back, smiling quietly at them all.

'Well?' Beth asked Tristan. 'What do you think?'

'Yes,' Tristan said thoughtfully. 'It certainly appears to be broken.'

I could not stifle a laugh.

'I know that, Tristan,' Beth snapped. 'Can you fix it?'

Tristan closed the door.

'I'll get my tools and see.'

While Tristan went off, Beth began to unload the spoiled foodstuffs.

'We'd better pull this away from the wall,' she said. 'It might be nothing more than the plug needs rewiring.'

I grabbed one corner, and she grabbed the other, but the appliance simply would not budge.

'Try and get it low down,' I said. 'Maybe one of the corners is caught on a piece of lino or something.'

Changing our grip seemed to make no difference. Tristan returned, and added his efforts, but to no avail. The fridge was tottering over dangerously, but the base remained solidly in place.

'It's hardly fastened to the floor with bolts or something,' I said, sweating and out of breath. 'Even if it's not, the damn thing weighs a ton!'

'I help, Tristan?'

Dominic had appeared at the door. The other members of the group had become bored and were engaged in craft.

'I don't think you can do much here, Dominic,' I said. 'We need a truck or something to drag this baby loose.'

'I do it,' Dominic said cheerfully, and before any of us could stop him, he had crossed the floor in two steps, crouched low, stuck his fingers under the fridge and heaved.

Tristan and I moved simultaneously. As it had done before, the structure lurched forwards – the rear of the base seemed to be loose, while the front was definitely anchored on something – and if we had not been there, it would have fallen on top of Dominic.

'Let go, Dom,' I grunted. 'This is not going to work.'

As I said this, there was a loud tearing sound, and the entire body of the fridge slid towards us, the rear legs thudding back down onto the floor as the weight was redistributed.

'I did it!' Dominic giggled, continuing to pull until the whole thing was out in the middle of the kitchen.

'Dominic, you are a horse of a man,' Beth said.

I looked at the space which the fridge had occupied. A large chunk of linoleum and part of a floorboard had been ripped away. Tristan and I would have needed a crowbar to have moved it. Dominic simply stood up, brushed himself down and, still giggling, went back out to the group.

15

I ran into Leroy, Dominic's father, in the supermarket the Saturday after my first full week at Drumlin. He was a friendly, smiling man, and surprisingly short for someone who had produced a giant for a son. Dominic had inherited his height from his mother, Leroy informed me.

'He's a remarkable young man,' I said. We had stopped in the fruit and veg section. It was a busy afternoon and shoppers milled about us.

'Ah, he's a lovely young lad,' Leroy agreed. 'There's not a bad bone in him. He gets mixed up sometimes and makes mistakes, but he's so sweet-natured ... I worry about him sometimes, though.'

'Why?' I asked. It might seem like a stupid question, but I knew there were so many different reasons to worry about a child like Dominic, I couldn't even begin to guess what Leroy's particular concerns were.

'Dominic assumes everyone is good and will treat him fairly,' Leroy said. 'He's lucky in that we've always made sure he's around people who care about him and want to do right by him. When he's out, he doesn't look any different to anyone else, so he doesn't have people calling him the kind of names someone like Max has to constantly put up with. He takes everyone at face value.'

'And an awful lot of people can't be taken at face value,' I said.

'Exactly,' Leroy said. 'How do you explain duplicity to someone who has no concept of such a thing?'

I had no answer to that.

'I don't know,' I said. 'I don't think you can.'

Leroy smiled sadly, and picked up an apple from a tray of them to our left.

'He was always a special little boy,' he said. 'Even before.'

'Before the seizure that . . .'

Leroy nodded. 'My wife likes to say that Dominic was a normal child then, but he wasn't. There was always something a little bit different about him. Nothing major, nothing you could generally put your finger on, but it was there.'

I shook my head. 'How do you mean?'

'It's hard to explain,' Leroy said.

'Try.'

'When he was three years old,' Leroy said, 'Dominic went missing. He had never done that before. He was actually afraid of the road and the traffic, so we never bothered to get a padlock for the front gate. We were really surprised, and, as I'm sure you can imagine, horrified, when we discovered he wasn't in the back garden where he'd been playing. We searched everywhere we could think of, but finally, in panic, we called the gardaí.'

'You must have been beside yourselves,' I said.

'We were. The police conducted a thorough search and failed to find the child. Three hours had passed by now, and we were starting to think the worst – that someone might have snatched him. The word had spread by then, and the neighbours had gotten together and organized a search party. Would you believe, it was a ten-year-old boy from across the road who finally found him.'

'Where was he?'

'Perched on a branch of a tree in the back garden, fast asleep. He had apparently been there all afternoon. It was a favourite spot of his, but no one had thought to look. He told me later that he had watched us all coming and going, had seen the police, had heard us talking about the fact that he was gone and we couldn't find him, but had stayed exactly where he was.'

'Probably thought it was all a game,' I said.

Leroy smiled and patted me on the shoulder.

'I don't know of any other three-year-old who could keep a game of hide-and-seek up for three hours.'

As I watched him walk off through the crowd, I realized that I didn't know of such a child either. I also pondered, as I continued with my own grocery shopping, that the story Leroy had just told me indicated more than just a rose-tinted world view. It also pointed to a steely determination and a sense of self-sufficiency which Dominic's sweet exterior hid very well indeed.

16

The house seemed to nestle into the side of the mountain like a child seeking comfort from a huge, misshapen mother. If I had not known otherwise, I would have thought it derelict. What had probably once been a garden could be seen out front, now completely overgrown with heather and furze. The pathway had bracken growing through the paving stones, and the roof was so sunken in the centre I feared it might cave in. Tristan rolled down the car window and peered out. A light rain was beginning to fall.

'I think this has to be the place,' he said.

'Must be.'

'Come along then. Let's see what we can find.'

It was early afternoon. That morning, Tristan had called me into his office.

'This is Aisling Cowman,' he said, introducing me to an elderly woman with the bluest blue-rinse hair I had ever seen. 'She wishes to seek our assistance with a friend of hers.'

'I'm pleased to meet you,' I said.

'I want you to make Lonnie come to the centre here,' she said.

'Lonnie is your friend?' I asked.

'He is the son of Peggy Whitmore, who was a dear friend to me for many years. I did not learn that Lonnie even existed until after Peggy's death. I am sorry to say that she probably did not treat the lad well.'

'You didn't know she had a son?' I said. 'I thought this woman was your best friend.'

'She was. I met her when we both worked for the post and telegraph company in Dublin. We were room-mates. Then, when their father died, she returned to her home to live with her sister, and I lost touch with her for a few years, but when I came back here myself, we re-established contact. I visited her many times, and she came over to my home for dinner; we went shopping together and even on holiday on occasion. During all those years, she never once mentioned that she had a son.'

'How'd you find out, then?'

'Peggy and her sister lived in a big house on the Dublin road. I always thought it was too large for their needs, but they came from a wealthy family, and status was important to them. From what we can gather, Peggy had a heart attack one night, and when her sister found her, the shock killed her, too. They were discovered several days later by a man who used to do a few odds and ends about the garden for them. It was him who also found Lonnie. The poor boy was half-starved at that stage.'

'Where was he?' Tristan asked.

'They had made some room for him in the attic of the house. That's where he lived.'

'And he never went out?'

'From what I can gather, he never left those rooms at all. I think they were ashamed of him, so they kept him hidden.'

Tristan nodded. 'And he is physically disabled, you say?'

The old woman sighed. 'He's a midget.'

'He suffers from dwarfism?' I said, partly to correct her, and also to be clear. 'He's not just short?'

'No. He's built differently. He has a hunched back, and kind of bowed legs, and his arms are very long. He's strong, though. But sure, he's afraid of everything. He's scared of his own shadow.'

'And he still lives in the family home?' Tristan asked.

'No. They left him a cottage the family owned. It's on the other side of the mountain. He lives there. I bring him his meals, and make sure he's all right. I've tried getting him to go out, but he'll have none of it. Then someone told me about this place, so I thought I'd see if you might be able to help him. He's a lovely boy – well, he's not a boy at all, I just tend to think of him like that. He doesn't know what age he is, but he must be more than forty. Can you do something for him?'

'Give us directions,' Tristan said, 'and we'll see what we can do.'

Aisling rifled through her cavernous handbag. 'I drew ye a map,' she said.

We sat and looked at the cottage, which was like something from a dark fairytale.

'I cannot fucking believe those old biddies would lock a child away because he was disabled,' I said. 'I mean, you hear about things like that in old stories from the history books – kings and queens walling up princes who were born with deformities and would be seen as a slur on the royal lineage – but I didn't think it happened in reality.'

'There is a long history in Ireland of such things,' Tristan said. 'People often see a disabled child as a punishment from God. Some men feel it is a slur on their virility – how could I be a real man if I can't sire a healthy child. Look at Irish folklore and the legends of changelings – creatures left behind by the fairies. That old tale was used as a way of getting rid of countless children with disabilities. The accepted wisdom was that you had to let the changeling know you were on to it, and it would then have to leave your house. You scalded it with hot water, put it on hot coals, beat it with a blackthorn stick, held it under water and drowned it. These children were tortured to death, and it was all seen as perfectly reasonable conduct.'

'This is the twenty-first century, Tristan. We're supposed to have evolved.'

'People don't really change. The stories become more scientific and the excuses more convoluted, but the fears are just the same.'

81

The front door was made of dark varnished wood, which was cracked and peeling. Tristan knocked. There was no response, just the sound of the wind whistling through the ancient oak trees that grew about the little house. Somewhere on the mountain I heard a lark singing. Tristan knocked again. Still nothing.

'I had hoped we wouldn't have to do this,' he said, taking a key Aisling Cowman had given us from his pocket.

'If he's jumpy, we're going to scare the living daylights out of him,' I said.

'There's no hope for it; we're going to have to go in,' Tristan said.

He slotted the key into the rusty lock, and turned it.

The smell that came out of the dark hallway was of rotten food, dust and sweat. Inside, I could see woodchip wallpaper with lots of religious paraphernalia hanging over it. The passage seemed to end in a T-junction, and there was an open doorway at the end, facing us.

'Lonnie, my name is Tristan Fowler, and this is my colleague, Shane Dunphy. Your friend Aisling asked us to come and have a chat with you.'

Still no response.

'D'you think he popped out for a drink?' I suggested.

'He's supposed to be agoraphobic,' Tristan said, 'so I think it unlikely.'

We moved slowly down the hallway. The door at the end opened onto a living room, which was in complete darkness, except for a television, which was switched to horse racing, providing the only source of light. I stepped inside. The furniture consisted of a coffee table, on which sat several plates with semi-congealed food upon them, some of which supported a healthy crop of green mould; a threadbare couch and two uncomfortable-looking armchairs. The mantelpiece was loaded with more religious trinkets: a plastic dome with an elaborate statuette of the Blessed Virgin, complete with a crown so tall it would have caused a spinal injury if she were a real person, several crucifixes and many of those laminated cards with portraits of saints on one side and prayers on the other. I went over to open the curtains to allow some light in when I heard a gurgling snarl, and something landed on my back.

'What the fuck!' I said, but the rest of my words were cut off as I felt hands closing about my windpipe.

Instinctively, I dropped to my knees on the carpet amidst all the dust-devils and some old tabloid newspapers, and tried to throw my assailant over my head. This only resulted in one hand letting go of my neck (its fellow simply tightened even more) and the other grasping my hair. I managed to get my own fingers under those about my throat and pried them loose when a cry brought everything to a standstill: 'Stop this at once! Let him go immediately!'

I heard steps coming up rapidly behind me, and then the weight was gone and I was taking deep breaths of the stale air. I heaved myself up onto one of the armchairs and came face to face with my opponent, who was glaring at me venomously.

'You can't come in here,' he croaked. 'This is my house.'

Lonnie was probably just under four feet tall, most of which was made up of a long, muscular torso. His legs were short and bowed, but looked strong. He had broad shoulders, one of which had a large hump, which rose almost above his right ear. His hair was long, curly and dark, greying at the tips. He had a heavy brow and a roman nose, and his eyes were deep-set and powerfully intelligent.

'You come in here, I'll fight you,' he said again, raising his fists. He would have come at me again, if Tristan hadn't shouted.

'Mr Whitmore, we were asked to come and speak with you, and given the key because Aisling did not believe you would let us in when we knocked. As it happens, she was right. Now please do not attack Shane again, or I shall have to restrain you.'

Lonnie moved back, and hopped up on the couch. He was still not happy, and fidgeted as he waited to hear what Tristan had to say. When the sales pitch for Drumlin was finished, the little man grunted. 'Okay. You talked, I listened. You go now.'

'I'd like you to come and see the unit,' Tristan said. 'I think you might just enjoy yourself.'

'No. Not going. This is my house. I'm happy here.'

'Aren't you lonely?' I asked, coming back to myself a little.

'You shut up,' Lonnie shot back at me.

'No, I won't,' I said. 'I wasn't rude to you, and I don't see why you feel you can be rude to me.'

'I'll punch you on your big fat nose,' Lonnie said, quite matter-of-factly. 'How would you like that?'

I wasn't sure what to say. I'm not small, and can hold my own in most physical situations, but I did not doubt for one second that this tiny, angry person would make good on his threat.

'That is quite enough,' Tristan said sharply. 'Now, one thing you will learn, Lonnie, is that I do not tolerate that type of behaviour. In Drumlin, you treat others with courtesy, or you are not welcome. I do not believe you think violence is appropriate. I would like to see you acting accordingly.'

Lonnie chuckled merrily, and clapped his hands in glee. 'You're funny fellas,' he said in his strange guttural manner. 'And we've all had a nice visit and a bit of a laugh. But I don't want none of what you're selling.'

Tristan motioned at me with his head. I stood up.

'All right. We'll leave you to your solitude. But I would like you to at least think about what I've said.'

Lonnie remained seated. 'Maybe,' he said.

'So what did you make of Lonnie?' Tristan asked as we drove home in his Citroën.

'I think that dude thinks he's much taller than he is,' I said, rubbing my throat.

'He does, doesn't he?' Tristan said. 'And that gives us something very useful to work with.'

That evening, as the clients all queued to climb onto the bus which would take them home, a filthy tractor, which had some random bits of red paint showing here and there through the mud that caked it, rolled up outside, and the enormous figure of William Kelleher unfolded itself from the seat.

He seemed to be wearing the same overalls he'd had on when I met him that night at his home. I was struck yet again by the raw, glowering presence of the man. Annie, who had been just about to get onto the bus, stepped back down, and skulked over to him. He had still not said a word, just stood, waiting for her to come to him. Tristan, who had been sitting in the driver's seat of the bus, hopped out, and went over to the enormous man.

'William, nice to see you. We haven't had the pleasure in quite some time.'

Annie's father did not look at Tristan. 'Been busy.'

'Your daughter is a constant joy to us,' Tristan said. 'She is quite a talented young woman, you know.'

'She's simple,' William said in his rumbling baritone.

'She sees the world in a different way to you and I, but that doesn't make her any less of a person,' Tristan said, gently.

'Mmm. She helps me about the farm, at least,' William growled. 'I need her now.'

'There she is,' Tristan said. 'It was nice of you to drop by.'

William Kelleher said not another word, just squeezed himself back into the ancient vehicle. Annie put one foot on the step and hung onto the back of her father's chair, and off they went.

'Warm fella,' I said when Tristan came back over.

'He's a cold one, all right.'

'Yet she seems happy, most of the time.'

'Annie is a free spirit,' Tristan said. 'Even the darkness he carries about with him can't contain her.'

'And thank God for that,' I said.

17

Max was having a bad day. Which meant everyone was having a bad day.

During news he belittled every single comment anyone made, and when Elaine started to tell us about a visit to the dentist the day before, where she had exhibited particular bravery in the face of many needles and pointed implements, he decided to start singing 'The Whole of the Moon' by the Waterboys at the top of his voice. When Beth took the group for a cookery lesson, in which she demonstrated a simple recipe for chicken curry, Max decided it would be a good idea to pour sugar into the pot when her back was turned, and the entire dish was rendered inedible. During art he drew a series of phalluses in various colours and of various sizes. I suggested to Millie that this might be a Freudian thing, and she retorted that perhaps Max was going through the 'arsehole complex'. When no one paid any attention to his efforts, Max grabbed a brush and started to paint a penis in bright yellow on the wall. Tristan removed the brush from his hand and stood over him until the image was cleaned off.

Lunch proved even more challenging. An important reason for us all to eat together was so the clients could mirror the correct table manners of the staff. Max spent the entire meal wandering from place to place, a chunk of a sandwich clutched in his fist.

'This is really regressive behaviour,' Valerie said to me. 'I haven't seen him like this in ages.'

'What do you think set him off?' I wondered.

'Probably something at home,' she said. 'His mum drinks,

so maybe she fell off the wagon. Oh, we'll find out sooner or later. He tells us everything, eventually.'

The afternoon proved just as difficult. The group was to go to the gym, but Tristan, wisely, felt that Max was too much of a risk in a facility with weights and other implements that could either be damaged, or used to do damage to others. As insurance dictated that Tristan had to be on site when Drumlin used the gym (among all his other skills, Tristan was a qualified physical trainer) we had to draw straws to determine who would stay with our errant friend. As I had suspected would happen, I drew the short straw.

'So, what do you want to do this afternoon, then?' I asked, when the others were gone.

Max was striding up and down by the far wall, banging a table with his fist every now and again, bouncing on the balls of his feet in a show of how wound up he was. He shot me a look at the question, but didn't answer.

'Last chance to tell me, Max,' I said. 'If you want to come up with an idea, great. If not, well, I've got stuff to do and you can amuse yourself.'

'F . . . fuck off,' Max said.

'Your call.' I shrugged, and sat down to write up a report on Tristan's and my visit to Lonnie the previous day.

Max made his way to the reading corner and threw himself on a beanbag. Ten minutes later, I heard an intermittent thump, thump, thump. Looking up, I saw that he was tossing books off their shelves on to the floor.

'You can knock yourself out doing that, Max,' I said. 'But you *will* put them back when you're done.'

Thump, thump, thump.

I looked back down at my report and decided to leave him to it. Five minutes later a book sailed through the air and hit me *smack* on the top of my head. It didn't hurt so much as surprise me. But that was it: I would have to go over and deal with Max. He stood to meet me as he saw me approach, his face flushed and his fists balled.

'Max, if you are trying to be a pain in the arse, you have well and truly succeeded,' I said.

Pop!

I didn't see the punch coming – but it was a beauty. Max must have balanced himself well, and he managed to put all his considerable weight behind the blow. It connected squarely with my jaw, and lifted me completely off my feet. I sailed backwards and – at least there was one positive in the whole affair – landed with a soft thud on a beanbag. Bells rang. Stars wheeled before my vision. I was vaguely aware of scuffling movement, and by the time my head cleared, Max was nowhere to be seen.

I pulled myself up and checked the kitchen, the office and the bathrooms, but there was no sign of him. I went to the door, which was standing ajar. Max's bicycle was gone, and so was he. I walked out to the road, and could just see a figure that I took to be him disappearing into the distance. I rubbed my jaw, which I could already feel swelling.

'You're going to have a bruise on that,' a voice said.

Startled, I looked down to see Lonnie Whitmore scowling up at me. 'When did you get here?' I asked.

'Just as the mongoloid boy was running out.'

'We don't use that word,' I said.

'Why not?'

'It's offensive.'

'Why?'

'Would you like it if I called you a dwarf?'

'Why would I care? I am a dwarf. I've been called worse.'

He was not dressed to avoid attention. He had a wide-brimmed red slouch hat on his head, and a green cape-coat that trailed along the ground after him. Under his arm was a brightly coloured floral shopping bag. He had a pink umbrella in his other hand, which he carried across the shoulder that was not hunched.

'Well, the right way to talk about someone like you is to say a "little person" or a "person of small stature".'

Lonnie laughed. 'Snow White and the Seven Persons of Small Stature? It'll never catch on,' he said.

I had to laugh, too. 'No. I don't suppose it will.'

'Is the grey-haired fella here?'

'No. They've gone out. He'll be back later, though.'

'When?'

'In an hour or so.'

'Can't wait. Tell him I called.'

'Why don't you come in and wait?'

Lonnie considered this for a moment.

'Because I don't really like you,' he said, and, turning on his heel, headed back towards town.

Convinced that volunteering at Drumlin might just have been the worst decision I had ever made, I went back inside and found some frozen peas to put on my jaw.

I told Tristan about Lonnie's visit when he got back, and also about Max's departure, leaving out the details of my first-round knockout. My jaw was red, but my beard covered most of it, so out of simple embarrassment I thought I'd keep that little nugget of information to myself. We were all having a mid-afternoon cup of tea before the final module of the day.

'And Lonnie didn't feel like waiting?' Tristan enquired.

'No.'

'It was quite a thing for him to come at all,' he said, sounding pleased. 'We must have made more of an impression than we thought.'

'I know. I'm not sure he's as terrified of everything as Aisling thinks.'

Tristan thought about that. 'The truth is probably some-where in the middle,' he said. 'He's been locked away for so

90

long, it'll take time for him to get used to being around people.'

'Will he fit in here?' I asked. 'I mean, he doesn't seem to have an intellectual disability, per se.'

'Don't get caught up in seeing disability so two-dimensionally. From the newspapers and prayer books and things in his house, it's obvious that Lonnie can read, and he seems to have at least an average vocabulary. But his social skills are sorely lacking, and I would have severe doubts that he could do some basic tasks like doing his own shopping, or going into a café.'

'I'd say you're right there.'

'So you see, disability comes in all shapes and sizes.'

'In this case, it comes in the shape of one mean little guy, with very odd fashion sense.'

Tristan looked at me questioningly.

'You'll see, if he ever comes back,' I said, and went to set up the last module of the day, which was art.

We were completing our map of the town's main street. Elaine and I were working on her contribution, a florist's shop which would fit in about midway down the street. It was a lovely building, in actuality – an old town house from the nineteenth century, which had been maintained with the original brick-work and windows.

Because the finished map (if you could call it that – portrait might be a better description) was going to be so large, we had spread our work across the entire room, with all the tables covered. Elaine and I had found a spot on the floor.

The project was being completed in a variety of materials and media. Elaine had gone to great lengths to press flowers for the window boxes of her piece, and she was now painstakingly gluing each one on. I had to admit that she had an amazing eye for colour. The picture was shaping up to be really beautiful.

The room was a buzz of activity. Our newly repaired radio

was playing some light classical music Tristan had found, and everyone was happily busy with their projects. Everyone except Dominic, that is.

'My daddy picking me up at four o'clock,' he declared every five minutes or so.

Valerie was working with him, but it seemed she was doing most of the work.

'Come on, Dominic,' she urged. 'This is supposed to be your shop, not mine.'

'I. Am. Tired,' Dominic said firmly, and put his head down on the table.

'Well, don't you dare complain if you don't like what I'm doing here,' Valerie said.

'My daddy picking me up at four o'clock,' Dominic said resolutely, and continued to sit with his chin on his hands, his eyes fixed on the door.

I was only peripherally aware of Dominic's protestations, and had more or less forgotten about him when the door opened, and Leroy came in.

'Must be four o'clock,' I said to Elaine, who looked up, spotted Leroy, and said: 'Leroy always picks Dominic up at four o'clock,' without any sense of irony.

'There's my daddy,' Dominic said, as if this vindicated him fully.

'Hello, Dominic,' Leroy said, grinning at his son.

Seeing as he already had his coat on in preparation for his departure, the lad flung back his chair and strode straight for the door. Unfortunately his rapid trajectory brought him right past where Elaine and I were working.

I have long hair – have had since I was a teenager. If I am doing something physical, or working with a child or an adult who is going to be potentially violent, I tie it back in a ponytail, but the rest of the time, I wear it down. Doing a piece of art hardly ranks as physical, so my hair was loose – this proved to be very much to my detriment.

Dominic swept past us on his relentless path toward his dad and home. As he did, one of the buttons of his duffel coat somehow managed to get tangled in my hair. I noticed immediately, and jerked backwards, calling: 'Hey, Dominic, hold up there a mo,' but my young friend was not to be stopped.

'I. Am. Going. Home,' he said, and kept going, not slowing his pace one iota.

Before I could do anything to prevent it, I was being dragged across the floor by my hair. I would like to say I handled this indignity manfully. It would be nice if I could report that I stoically held out until somebody detached me. But neither of these things would be even close to the truth. In reality, I howled.

'Dominic, my hair!' I shouted. 'Stop, for fuck's sake!'

Dominic, still moving forwards at exactly the same momentum, looked over his shoulder, saw me, and giggled.

'I didn't do it!' he said, and kept going.

I felt my hair starting to rip at the roots. Thankfully, Leroy had rushed over by this time and stopped his son. A little quick surgery with a pair of scissors, and I was free, if with yet another aching spot to show for my day's work. Dominic was completely unapologetic.

'I done nothing,' he said, and swept out the door.

18

Max was waiting at the gate the next morning when I arrived looking tearful and chastened. As he didn't say hello, or sorry, or try to punch me out again, I ignored him and went on inside.

Turning up to the unit that day had not been easy. My initial thoughts had been to call Tristan and tell him I had reconsidered my situation, and that it was just not working out. After all, my reason for volunteering in the first place was to leave a back door to escape through if necessary.

But then, I had received the occasional thump before in the line of work, and I knew that I had not done anything wrong in the way I had dealt with Max. He had never been violent towards anyone in Drumlin since I had started going there, so I'd had no reason to be wary of him. I thought I'd face the music.

Despite the fact that I was quite clear that what had happened was not my fault, I still felt like an idiot. Part of me thought I should have been able to avoid it in some way. I was just glad no one had seen me getting the hiding.

News proved to be the nightmare I expected it to be. As soon as Millie declared the session to be open, Max raised his hand.

'Me talk.'

'Okay, Max.'

With a trembling lower lip, he went around the group, naming everyone in turn: 'Millie, Beth, Tristan, Glen, Elaine, Annie, Dominic . . .'

When everyone had been acknowledged, Max put his head into his hands, and moaned. 'Yesterday, me not feeling very good in myself.'

'I think we were all aware of that, Max,' Tristan said.

'Was mean to Elaine in news.'

'You were mean,' Elaine agreed.

'Drew dirty pictures,' Max continued.

Every single trespass was listed. If I was a cynical man, I might have thought Max was getting a certain degree of entertainment out of recalling his litany of offences. As was inevitable, he reached his final transgression: 'I boxed Shane.' As he said it, he made a punching motion in the air.

'Yes, I see he has something of a crumpled look this morning,' Tristan said, suppressing a smile. 'Hit him hard, did you?'

'Boxed him in the face,' Max said, and I felt myself flushing redder by the minute. 'Knocked him down.' He illustrated this in the air with his finger, whistling to demonstrate me sailing through the air, and then making an exploding noise as I impacted.

'And did you say sorry to him?' Tristan asked.

'No,' Max said. 'Me ran off.'

'I see,' Tristan said. 'I think you have some work to do, young man, don't you?'

Max nodded. 'Want to say sorry to the group,' he said. 'Let meself down. Let all of you down.'

'Okay. And I think there's someone else who deserves a special apology,' Tristan said.

Max stood up, and looked at me. 'Shane,' he said, and burst into tears. With his arms wide, he rushed over and gave me a bear hug.

I didn't know what to do. I did not believe for one moment that this apology was even vaguely genuine, but Max had stage-managed his performance so well, I was trapped into accepting his theatrics – and I had had no time to think about a more appropriate response. Max broke off the hug, and went back to his seat, sniffling and wiping his eyes, but looking extremely smug. I sat where I was, feeling thoroughly used and not a little bit stupid. For all that Max was supposed to be the one with the intellectual disability, he had outsmarted me brilliantly.

One of the parts of the programme that happened every day without fail – and sometimes more than once – was called craft. Tristan explained to me that there were good reasons that it formed a bedrock of what was done at Drumlin, as the various skills it involved (everything from weaving to woodwork, embroidery to etching) helped develop fine motor skills (all those little, precise movements), hand–eye co-ordination, not to mention concentration over an extended project. The problem I had was that, no matter how hard I tried, I just didn't like craft, and had absolutely no talent for it.

When it became obvious that I had no real patience with making things out of wood, and that I found weaving simply too tedious for words, Tristan decided to try me on something different. Glen had been expressing a desire to try Airfix modelling for a while, and Tristan thought this might be something I would enjoy. I put it to him that I had never gotten much of a kick out of the endeavour when I was a kid, and therefore thought it unlikely I would now, but in the spirit of goodwill, I said I'd give it a go.

Glen and I made our way into the biggest toy shop in town, and the red-haired youngster picked out a large plane. Now, it had a much fancier name than that, and there was a huge amount of information that came with it about what it had been used for in whichever war it had been used in, but as far as I was concerned, it was a big plane. The man in the shop informed us that everything we needed was in the kit, and off we went. Glen was anxious to get started as soon as we got back to the unit.

'It's a cool plane,' he said. 'I am reminded strongly of the plane in one of my favourite movies, *Con Air*, with Nicholas Cage and John Cusack. Although that was a passenger plane used to carry dangerous criminals, and this is a war plane used for dropping bombs in pre-decided military targets, but I think you see where I'm making the connection.'

'I do.'

'There was a series of films made in the nineteen seventies featuring planes as central plot devices. I am, of course, referring to the spoofs made by the Zucker brothers, starring Leslie Nielsen and Lloyd Bridges, called *Airplane*. There were also a number of films of a more serious nature, which featured the acting skills of George Kennedy, called the *Airport* series. Now, these were classified as disaster movies – but I think they were quite successful.'

Our modelling project proved to be something of a disaster. After our first session, we both had to be unstuck from the fuselage of the model – luckily Beth had foreseen this possibility, and had the correct materials to do the job. It took us two more periods of work to get the item finished, and certainly, the results did look vaguely like a plane, but probably not one that could have ever flown.

'It's not exactly what you'd call streamlined, now is it?' Tristan asked. 'And I don't think we're supposed to be able to see globs of dried glue.'

'Shane says it's an impressionistic view of a plane,' Glen said, proudly.

'That's one way of looking at it,' Tristan agreed. 'Aren't the wings supposed to be pointing in the other direction?'

I was permitted to find something else to do during craft after that. I was a volunteer, after all.

PART 5

'Where Do You Go To, my Lovely?'

Wild nights. Wild nights!
Were I with thee,
Wild nights should be
Our luxury!

Futile the winds
To a heart in port,
Done with the compass,
Done with the chart.

Rowing in Eden!
Ah, the sea!
Might I but moor
To-night with thee!

'Wild Nights' by
Emily Dickinson

19

Tristan was a pathological photographer. There was not a single occasion that did not, in Tristan Fowler's mind, warrant getting out the camera and taking roll after roll of film to preserve the memory of it for those who may come afterwards. I have to admit, I found this entire process deeply irritating, but there was nothing for it but to freeze and smile on command when my new boss decided he wanted to catch me in a candid moment (I tried to explain that smiling for the camera made the shot slightly less than candid, but he would hear none of it).

As a result of this, there was a cupboard in Tristan's office full to bursting with box after box of photos, dating back to the time he and Beth were still working for the centre attached to the church. One evening after work, Tristan decided to go through his collection, with a mind to putting some of the shots into albums, or maybe even framing them.

'They're a history of the unit, after all,' he informed me. 'It's a pity to have them all shut away like that.'

The real problem with sorting through all the snaps and putting them into any kind of order was that they were thoroughly jumbled, with no markings whatsoever to suggest when or even where they had been taken. Day trips to various locales, sports days, birthday parties, dramatic performances, all these were bundled together with no categorization applied at all. The only thing for it was for Beth, Tristan and I to simply hold up picture after picture, while they each tried to establish a vague timeline.

An hour later, I opened up a packet of photos, and the first one immediately caught my eye. It was of a group of people lined up against a wall, smiling inanely for the camera: a classic Tristan Fowler pose. What particularly attracted my attention to this shot was that among the group there was only one person I could recognize – Dominic. It was obviously taken several years ago – I guessed at the church-based setting – and Dominic seemed a little shorter and a little more slender.

What really caused me to stop and stare, though, was the fact that Dominic, who must have been around twelve or thirteen years old, was sucking a child's pacifier. I looked at the photograph from all angles to make sure that I was correct, and not seeing something else – a sweet or something – but I was not. Dominic was sucking a pink dummy.

I held up the photo.

'What's the story here?'

Tristan squinted across the table at the shot.

'Well, I would say that needs to go into the pile over beside Beth.'

'Why is Dom sucking a dummy?'

Beth did not even look up.

'He used to when he started with us. It took us nearly two years to break the habit. He loved his dodie, that's for sure. Gave it up kicking and screaming. At times literally.'

I could not believe what I was hearing.

'But he was what – thirteen then? I mean, who in the name of God thought it was a good idea to give the kid a soother? That's like setting him up to have the piss taken out of him!'

Tristan looked at me over the rims of his glasses.

'Do you think Dominic is stupid, Shane?'

'No.'

'And do you think Leroy or his wife are cruel people?'

'No.'

'Well then, why would you assume that Dominic would use his soother anywhere he would be likely to receive negative attention for it? Or that Leroy would permit him to do so?'

'So he only had it here or at home?' I said.

'Precisely.'

I considered that.

'I still don't like it.'

'Neither did we,' Beth said, 'which is why he doesn't use it any more.'

'But why did he in the first place?'

'Have you heard of regression therapy?' Tristan asked.

'I have.'

'As you know, then, when a child misses out on a stage of their development through abuse or neglect, psychologists will sometimes suggest that they revisit that period, even when they are much older. So you will have teenagers being bottle-fed and so on.'

'I know all that,' I said. 'Dominic didn't miss out on anything, surely.'

'He did not. In his case he returned to a previous stage of development and stayed there. Dominic, in a lot of ways, is a two-year-old. He enjoys soft toys and the *Teletubbies* and a good soother.'

'But he's *not* two!' I said. 'It's disrespectful to allow him to behave like that.'

'To his parents, Dominic had gone back to being a baby,' Beth said, 'How do you refuse a baby the basic comforts it enjoys?'

'That is one of the many tough parts of having a child with an intellectual disability,' Tristan said. 'While they grow up physically, mentally they reach a point and just ... stop. But you're absolutely right. We have to ensure they have the best chance available, and that means they need to take on some of the trappings of adulthood. Dominic is as much an adult as he can be. The way he dresses, and sometimes behaves, are all age appropriate.'

I looked at the photo again. There was something disturbing about it.

'Poor guy,' I said.

'Nicely taken shot though,' Tristan said, and went back to his sorting.

20

Three months passed. My life began to fall into a pattern: I would get up early and go for a run, have breakfast and then drive the ten miles to Drumlin. I was still living on the money from my gigging, so I didn't diminish the amount I was doing, but I did cap the number at five per week. If I was not out playing, I spent my evenings reading, writing or watching old movies. Glen was constantly referring to some movie or other, and despite the fact that I considered myself something of a film expert, his knowledge left me standing. Through his informed ramblings, I educated myself.

Lonnie started to come to Drumlin in the afternoons. Despite the fact that he was not half as frightened of the world as Aisling had suggested to us, nor nearly as aggressive (or rude) as he wanted to make out, he admitted begrudgingly that it took him the entire morning to pluck up the courage to come in to the unit. Despite our rocky beginnings, I found I liked him very much, and his acerbic wit and determination not to ever be seen as anything less than a full person endeared him to me even further.

Yet there was a pain and a sadness behind the gruff façade that I sensed from time to time. Even when he was joking, or being purposely obtuse about something, I knew this was a defence mechanism. Very quickly, we all learned that his method of interacting was to adopt a role with each of us. Tristan he referred to as the 'Captain' – any request was met with a salute and a 'Sir, yes, sir!' Tristan went to great pains to inform him that he had in fact been a gunnery sergeant during his time in the military, but to Lonnie, he was always the captain.

Ricki he called the 'little lady', and he always behaved in a ridiculously chivalrous manner towards her, opening doors, standing whenever she entered the room, bowing low, complimenting her at every turn. Ricki, for her part, lapped it up. The two seemed to have an immediate understanding and rapport that was lovely to see.

He continued his adversarial attitude to me, but within a day or so I understood that it was now meant in fun. Lonnie grasped every opportunity to make fun of me or to get a dig in, and I made sure to strike back every bit as enthusiastically. He would stand on the table so everyone could see him, holding a guitar he had cut out of cardboard, a fake beard made of cotton wool stuck to his face, and pretend to be me, singing. I would ask him when he came in each afternoon if he had got dressed in the dark (he seemed to perversely choose the most bizarre combinations of colours and styles). But I also learned that he could be fiercely protective of those he cared about and this extended to me, too.

One day, Glen and I were discussing the old, British-made Amicus horror movies. Amicus was a film company that operated parallel to Hammer, but at a considerably cheaper cost. Glen was speaking about a particular scene in one of the movies (*Dr Terror's House of Horrors*), where a disembodied hand (which once belonged to Christopher Lee) is haunting Michael Gough. Glen started to act out the hand creeping through the air, when Lonnie came in. Seeing Glen stalking towards me, his hand like a claw, Lonnie assumed the worst, and before I knew what was going on had leapt up on a chair and launched himself at the hapless Glen, who was too stunned to even defend himself.

Before any real harm was done, I grabbed Lonnie by the scruff of the neck and hauled him off. 'Jesus, Lonnie, take it easy,' I said, urgently. 'We were just play-acting.'

'I was being Christopher Lee's hand,' poor Glen said with feeling.

Lonnie straightened his shirt (a ruffled, lime-green affair). 'Yeah, well, I just didn't want anyone else killing you before I got the chance,' he said. 'I've got my own plans in that department.'

'Yeah, well, if you're going to cut my throat, you'd better wait until I'm lying down, or you'll never be able to reach,' I said.

'The taller they are, the harder they fall,' Lonnie said. 'But then, you're not *that* tall, really.'

'You can talk,' I said. 'You're the only person in Drumlin who needs a high chair at meal times.'

And so it went.

With Lonnie coming in regularly, and Meg now a more constant presence too since her disclosure, Tristan decided he needed to increase the staff ratio. When I assured him again that I did not want to be put on the payroll, he placed an advertisement in the local paper.

The result arrived to Drumlin a month later.

Her name was Sukie Boyle. She was twenty-three years old, fresh out of college, and she was gorgeous: long blonde ringlets; bright blue eyes; a full figure; as pretty as a summer sky.

That first morning, as we sat in our group for news, it was very difficult to remain focused on the task at hand. Sukie, for reasons best known to herself, seemed to think it appropriate to come in to work dressed as if she were going to a nightclub. She wore high-heeled shoes, a short skirt, and a top that left little to the imagination. Max, Glen, Dominic, and, admittedly, Tristan and myself, had to make a concerted effort to keep our eyes at face level. Or, rather, Tristan and I did. The others didn't even bother.

As the day went on, I saw Max acting out the same behaviour he had with me that first day, except this time he seemed to require lengthy hugs every few minutes, too. I shook my head in wonderment at how I could ever have fallen for Max's routine, but I also remembered how nervous and uncertain I was when I started at Drumlin, and reasoned that Sukie must be feeling much the same way.

At the end of that day, Tristan did a group exercise with us, which involved the person to your right reading you a list of objects they had in their shopping bag, and then you had to list as many back as you could, while adding one, which they had to remember the next time round. Everyone got a turn at reading and remembering, and Tristan kept moving the group about to mix up the pairs. When it came my turn to read, I found myself sitting opposite Sukie. I was about to start reading from the list in my hand, when she said, 'You don't remember me, do you?'

I stopped, and looked at her.

'Should I?'

'You taught me sociology and child protection when I was in first year at college. It was quite a few years back, now.'

'This was in the city?'

'Yeah. You probably don't remember. I had short hair, then, and glasses . . .'

I tried to remember the classes I had taught, but I drew a blank.

'I'm sorry. I must have seemed very rude when you came in.'

'No, you're grand. I was very quiet. I don't think I ever actually spoke to you.'

'Well, welcome to Drumlin.'

'Thanks. Any hints or tips for a raw beginner?'

I laughed. 'Well, maybe one.'

'What?'

'You're . . . um . . . not really dressed for the occasion, if you don't mind my saying so.'

'Am I not?'

'You look lovely, don't get me wrong. It's just that, well, I suppose you might think about showing a little less?'

'What?' Her voice was getting shrill, and I was beginning to get a little shrill myself.

'Jesus, this isn't coming out right at all,' I said. I decided the only thing to do was revert back into teacher mode. 'Think of it like this: there's no uniform here — you don't have to wear a smock or a particular pair of shoes, but, in a way, there *is* a uniform. Now, supposing we were going for a walk today, which we do sometimes. Do you remember Froebel, from college?'

'Sort of . . .'

'He's the guy who came up with the Kindergarten Method. Or Vygotsky?'

'I hated him.'

'Well, what both of those guys said was that getting a sense of where you come from is really, really important for you to know who you are. Also, there's a concept in the whole area of special needs. Have you ever heard of "maximum positive visibility"?'

'I might have . . .'

'It was originally put forward by Dr Barnardo, but I've heard others claiming it as their own. At any rate, it says that for a society to truly accept people with disabilities, they need to be seen going about their communities, accessing services, shopping, doing all the stuff that so-called normal people do. Here, we achieve that by going out as much as we can.'

'Yeah, I get that,' Sukie said.

'Right. Well, with those stilettos you're wearing today, I don't think you'd get very far.'

'I can walk really comfortably in these!'

'I don't doubt it. But what kind of distance can you travel?'

'Well . . .'

'Not too far, I'd guess. Now, also, whether we like it or not, Dominic and Max and Glen and Lonnie, and even some of the girls, are sort of confused about their sexuality. You know that when you dress like you are right now, it sends out certain messages to members of the opposite sex. You are showing how attractive you are – in anthropology, it's referred to as displaying.'

'Yeah but –'

'I'm not finished, Sukie. *I* know there are certain parameters around which you must act in civilized society. So does Tristan. I think Lonnie does, too, even though he sometimes chooses not to observe them. Max and Dominic, though, see, they can get a bit confused about things like that. Someone as . . . um . . . *womanly* as you are, looking the way you do today – it's liable to lead them into hassle they don't need.'

'I seem to remember you preaching that women should be able to dress how they like, when you were teaching us the history of feminism.'

'I'm all for dressing any way you please during your free time, Sukie. But when you're here, you're at work. That means you need to present a professional attitude. A mini-skirt and a tube-top might be professional dress if you're a model or a dancer or an actress or something, but it's not for a care worker. I mean, goddammit, hasn't social care struggled to be seen as a profession anyway? We don't need any more challenges to cope with, do we?'

'Sure you're only dressed in jeans and a T-shirt. I seem to remember you didn't exactly dress up when you were teaching, either.'

'If I need to climb a tree, or chase after someone who has run off, or restrain one of the lads after they've lost control, I can do it in what I'm wearing. I'd like to see you do a restraint in that get-up.'

'Well, pardon me, I'm sure,' Sukie said, and moved to the next seat along.

'Well, you did ask,' I muttered, and got on with the exercise.

21

The following day, Sukie was not speaking to me, but she was dressed modestly and sensibly in a tracksuit. Max and Glen seemed slightly disappointed.

Our new girl had asked to be permitted to do an activity she had designed with the group after lunch – some kind of relaxation exercise based on yoga, so I offered to do the washing-up. I found myself sharing the job with Beth. She laughed about Sukie's very obvious change in attire.

'Well, if you hadn't said it to her, I would have done,' Beth said. 'God almighty, what was she thinking?'

'Would it be very uncharitable to suggest that she was trying to impress the boss?' I said.

'Do you really think so?'

'Jesus, Beth, I don't know. Nothing else seems to fit.'

'Maybe she just wanted to look nice, and displayed, along with a lot of flesh –'

'I noticed.'

'I know you did – a genuinely unfortunate degree of immaturity. We all have to learn, Shane. You made your mistakes when you came, the same as anyone. None of us are immune to it.'

'And did you make your mistakes, Beth?'

'Of course. I mean, I started out in nursing, so mine were probably of a more medical nature. But yes, I messed up there, and when I found myself involved in working with people with disabilities, I messed up there, too, many times. I think that if I hadn't met Tristan, I'd still be messing up.'

'He's quite a guy.'

Beth smiled at that. 'He is quite the finest man I have ever met,' she said, without any sense of irony or embarrassment.

'You two work well together,' I said delicately.

'Oh yes, we've been a double act now for years.'

'It's great when you find someone you work well with,' I agreed. 'It can be a difficult thing, finding a pattern that works for you both.'

'Have you ever had that?'

'Yeah, from time to time. But I've always had itchy feet. Always felt the need to move on after a while, I suppose.'

'My husband was like that.'

I mulled over that one. There had never been a mention of a husband before.

'You were married?'

'I *am* married. He ran off on me a very long time ago. It's ancient history, now.'

'You never found anyone else?'

'Oh, there have been others, all right. But no one ever stuck around over the long haul.'

'I'm sorry to hear that.'

'Ah, don't be.' She laughed – but it was a sad laugh. 'I mean, sometimes it gets lonely, all right. I remember one New Year's Eve, I decided not to go out. It was shortly after we'd started Drumlin, so I had very little money, anyway. Well, I'd bought a bottle of cheap plonk, and when those bells chimed, I suddenly realized that I had nobody to sing "Auld Lang Syne" with, or wish Happy New Year to. So I picked up the phone and rang Tristan. Now, don't ask me how I forgot, but Tristan is very much one of those early to bed, early to rise types, and he'd been in bed since around ten o'clock. Well, when he answered the phone, he read me the riot act for calling at such an ungodly hour. I mean, you just have to laugh about it now, looking back.'

I laughed, more because she was laughing than for any other reason. I didn't find the story funny. I thought it was very sad.

★

At home time, Sukie called me over.

'Hey, teacher.'

'Hey.'

'Does my outfit meet your approval today?'

I sighed. 'I'm sorry if I offended you yesterday,' I said. 'I didn't mean to. If I worded what I was trying to say badly – and I think I did – I really do apologize. Can we bury the hatchet and start again?'

She grinned. 'Tristan took me aside today, and told me – much more bluntly that you did – that he never wanted to see me dressed like that again on a work day. So I guess you did me a favour.'

'You're welcome, I think,' I said, trying to work out if what I had just heard was an apology or an expression of thanks.

'What are you doing tonight?'

'I am watching a movie called *Stage Fright*, a Hitchcock film – Jane Wyman, Marlene Dietrich, Richard Todd. It's a classic.'

'How would you like me to cook you dinner first?'

'Are you serious?'

'I want to apologize to you for being such a cow. And I really would like some advice on the ins and outs of this place.'

'You haven't said a word to me all day, Sukie, and now you want to make me dinner.'

'Look, I'm not coming on to you, you eejit,' she said. 'You have to eat, I have to eat, I could do with some pointers – I mean, for Christ's sake, you were giving me a full fucking lecture yesterday.'

'Okay. Where do you live?'

She told me, and I said I'd see her at seven.

Dinner proved to be spaghetti Bolognese and only partially cooked garlic bread – my host was just out of college, after all. Sukie had a reasonably pleasant flat in town, which she admitted she was having difficulty paying for.

'I think I'm going to have to get a room-mate if I'm going to keep this place,' she informed me. 'The salary is okay at Drumlin, but I'm at the very bottom of the scale.'

'I'm living way out in the country,' I told her. 'My rent is next to nothing. Which is probably just as well.'

She was dressed in new blue jeans and a white, man-tailored shirt. She wasn't wearing any make-up, which made her look very young, miles away from the vamp who had arrived at Drumlin the day before.

'Yeah, Millie told me you're just volunteering – what's that all about? I mean, you're way qualified, aren't you?'

I laughed. 'Probably overly so. I suppose you could say that I have far too much education, combined with a major time deficit.'

'Come again?'

'I wanted to do something just for me,' I said. 'Now, it is a situation that I have discussed at length with Tristan, so let's just leave it at that, shall we?'

'Fair enough,' she said.

'So what do you want to ask me about working at Drumlin, then?' I said. 'Not that I think I'll be of much help to you. I'm barely in the door myself.'

'There is one thing that's been bothering me about the place, but I'm not sure how to even articulate it. It's a little bit politically incorrect.'

'Well, it's only you and me here, and political correctness is often quite over-rated. Just ask Lonnie.'

She sat back and poured herself some more wine. I was driving, so I was on cola.

'Okay. Could you tell me what the point of it all is?'

'The point of what?'

'Drumlin. Doing what we do there.'

'It's supposed to be about making the lives of the clients better.'

'Do we?'

'Ask Ricki if her life is better. Get Meg to tell you what her days were like before she started going.'

'I know all that. It's a nice place to spend a few hours. But I mean really – over the long term. Where are all these people going? Is Dominic ever going to have a job? Is Glen going to get married? Could you see Max living on his own one day? What's the game plan, when it all boils down?'

'Jesus, you don't ask easy questions, do you?'

'No. Sorry. But it occurred to me yesterday: why bother? Are any of these people going to amount to anything in the greater scheme of things? Could they ever contribute anything to their communities? Aren't they just a drain on the country's resources if we're really, cruelly honest? Why do we expend time and energy and money in setting up places like Drumlin for them?'

'Do you mind if I smoke?' I asked.

'Do you mind going out on the balcony?'

'Not at all.'

We brought our drinks onto the small balcony, and I lit a Cuban cigar. A friend had brought me back a box of them when he had holidayed there several years before, and I usually forgot I even had them.

'What you're asking is one of the big questions about social care – why do we do it? It's likely that three quarters of the kids I've ever worked with are probably going to end up no better off than before I – or anyone else – got involved with them. I mean, I've just spent four years working in a place we called Last Ditch House because we knew the families we were dealing with were probably never going to improve very much. But you see, as a civilized society, we have a responsibility, I believe, to try and help those less fortunate than ourselves. That probably sounds very simplistic and trite, but that's quite honestly what I believe.'

'No, it's fair enough,' Sukie said. 'But I bet there's more to it than that.'

'There is. There's a girl I worked with once, Mina, her name is. She's got Down's Syndrome, and even though she comes from a family who are very well off, and who love her unequivocally, well, she's had some tough times. She wanted so much to be loved and accepted that she reached out to the wrong people – bad people. She nearly died.'

'Poor girl.'

'Mina was attending a workshop, where there were lots of people who meant well, but who perhaps didn't see just how amazing she was. But Mina made them see. She kept pushing, and telling her family she wanted more, and now she works as a teacher's assistant in a school for kids with special needs, and she's very happy. It took some time for her potential to be seen, but finally it was. Now, she *is* giving something back, and through the fact that her life was made better, she is improving the lives of many others.'

'Yeah, but –'

'Don't you see? Any of our lads could be a Mina. They all have the capacity to become so much more than society allows them to be.'

'Isn't that outrageously optimistic?' Sukie asked.

'A friend of mine told me a story once,' I said, blowing smoke rings. 'He was in prison, see, and they'd all been taken swimming. My friend was, at this time, very, very angry with the world and the way he'd been treated. He was full of rage and resentment, so much so that he was blind to almost anything. This day he was just doing length after length of the pool. The facility had been cleared, because of course the town council did not want the public coming anywhere close to all these dangerous criminals.'

'Understandably,' Sukie said.

'Well, Karl, my friend, had stopped to have a breather, when he spotted this other group being brought in up in the shallow end. They were a bunch of people with disabilities from a centre not unlike Drumlin. It seems having them mixing with rapists and murderers was okay.'

'Charming.'

'Isn't it? Well, Karl went back to his laps. He didn't much care who else was in the pool, as long as he was left alone. But when he stopped again for a break, he noticed one little guy, a kid of maybe ten or eleven, who was in the deepest part of the shallow end. Why Karl's attention was drawn to him was because he was moving in a very odd way and seemed to be going round and round in circles. My friend went a bit closer, out of curiosity, and he realized this kid only had one arm. It hadn't been amputated, he was like one of those kids whose mothers had taken thalidomide – his hand, which was pretty much useless, came out of his shoulder. Karl told me that he had a water wing on his other arm, so he was sort of lying crooked in the water, and he was swimming for all he was worth.'

'Good for him.'

'Absolutely. Karl had never had any contact with people with disabilities before, and none with children since he was one himself. But he said this kid just captivated him. He couldn't take his eyes off him. He told me that what struck him, like a punch in the gut, was the iron will he saw in that little boy. There he was, in way over his head, with a water wing encumbering him more than anything else, but by God, he was going to swim for all he was worth.'

I paused to tap some ash off the tip of my cigar.

'Do you understand what I'm saying, Sukie?'

'I think so.'

'Every single one of the lads in Drumlin have faced more challenges and had more shit thrown at them in their lives, than you or I could ever understand. Yet they abide. They take on the world with a smile and a spring in their step, and they give of themselves with a remarkable generosity. They all have it in them to make the lives of those they interact with better. Look at me, for example.'

'What about you?'

'When I came to Drumlin, I was a mess. I'd had a fairly horrendous run of luck, and I had run away from my life. I have to say that being around the guys has made me feel a hell of a lot better.'

'Really?'

'Really,' I said. 'The truth is, whatever is going on in Drumlin, it's a special place. They've got something happening there that is worth being a part of. I don't think I've ever seen a more active representation of true integration before. The fact is, in Drumlin there is true equality. All the barriers society puts up, all the prejudices and all the preconceptions we have, Tristan has stripped them all away.'

'And that's reason enough to work there?' Sukie said.

'It is for me,' I said. 'You'll have to decide whether or not it is for you.'

She smiled, and patted me on the arm.

'Thanks, teacher.'

'You're welcome. I hope you were listening carefully. I'll be asking questions later.'

22

I was woken the next morning by someone knocking loudly on my front door. Actually, knocking is too mild a word. They were hammering. When I didn't answer immediately, whoever it was moved to the window that looked out from my living room, and clattered on that.

'Okay, hold your horses, I'm coming!' I said, dragging myself out of bed and pulling on my dressing gown. I glanced at the clock on my phone as I went: it was seven a.m.

As I opened the door, my early-morning caller shoved his way in, knocking me aside.

'Where is she?' Max (for it was he) demanded, stomping up the hallway and into my kitchen.

'Where is who?' I asked, genuinely puzzled and not a little bit annoyed.

'Where Sukie?' he asked, coming right up and jabbing me in the chest.

'She's at her own house!' I said, starting to get angry. 'What the hell is wrong with you, Max? I'm not due in work for another two hours, and neither are you, so I'd appreciate it if you'd please get back on your bike and go home. Your mother will be worried sick.'

'Sukie my girlfriend!' Max said, standing firm and crossing his arms over his chest. 'She love me!'

'Sukie is not your girlfriend, and she barely even knows you, Max,' I said. 'I'm sure she likes you a great deal, but you are being unreasonable.'

'You go on a date with her,' he said, his mood becoming even more agitated.

'If I did, it would be none of your business, Max,' I said. 'But as it happens, I did not.'

'You go over her house last night,' Max was shouting now. 'I see you. I follow you.'

'You followed me?'

'On my bike.'

'You followed me on your bike? Are you out of your mind?' I asked.

'I hear her say to you she cook dinner. She say that yesterday.'

'Yes, she did. And I went over to her flat, and we had a nice evening, but she is not my girlfriend, Max. I am far too old for a girl like Sukie to be interested in. She's new and she's a little bit lonely here, and she wanted to talk, that's all.'

'You have her here!'

'No, I do not!' I said, shouting myself now. 'I want you to go, Max, before I get really annoyed.'

I saw the punch coming this time, and dodged it easily. As his fist went past me, I grabbed him by the elbow and spun him, so I had a grip from behind. With my hand in the small of his back I shoved and ran him out the front door, which was still open, before he had a chance to do anything about it.

'You and I will talk about this again, Max,' I called after him as he cycled away, cursing me loudly.

As it happened, Max did not arrive in to Drumlin that day, or the next. By the time he did return, I had other things on my mind.

PART 6

Every Blooming Thing

Now this is the law of the jungle, as old and as true as the sky,
And the wolf that shall keep it may prosper, but the wolf that shall
break it must die.

From *The Law of the Wolves* by Rudyard Kipling

23

I had taken to visiting Lonnie at weekends. He always pretended that my calling was a huge inconvenience, and clattered
about his little kitchen making tea and finding biscuits, but I
knew he was delighted. More often than not on a Friday,
just before leaving for the bus, he'd ask, 'I suppose you'll be
dropping in to make my place look untidy on Saturday?'

'Ah, I'll probably call over,' I'd respond. 'I think I'll bring
my own chair this time, though. Yours are all so teeny, I'm
afraid I'll break one of them on you.'

'You know there's a difference between tall and having a fat
arse, don't you?'

'Is that what they say in Lilliput? Bless.'

I wanted Lonnie to talk about his life before Drumlin. He
had ample reason to be angry, and there was a bubbling under-
current of rage in every word he uttered, yet it remained
unspoken, and I was afraid that if he did not get it out of
his system, it might get turned inward and destroy him. I was
also fascinated by the fact that he was so knowledgeable and
well read.

'The one thing I had plenty of all my life was books,' he
explained. 'My mother and my aunt had a huge library, and
they taught me to read very young. I can't remember not being
able to read, actually. They soon discovered that when I was
reading I was quiet, so they gave me any book I wanted.'

'What were your favourites?'

He shifted uncomfortably.

'You'll laugh.'

'Why would I laugh?'

He cleared his throat. 'I liked Tolkien.'

I could have kicked myself. Of course he'd love Tolkien. Here was a writer who had created an entire dwarf culture, and a network of diminutive characters who were as tough, as strong and as resilient as any of their taller associates.

'I love his stuff too. Have you seen the films?'

'Never much liked films. Only thing I ever really watch on telly is sport.'

'Fair enough. The books are always better anyway.'

'So I've heard.'

I talked to Tristan about my concerns the following Monday, and told him of a plan I had.

'He loves to read, and he loves fantasy stories,' I said. 'Maybe we could use that to get him talking.'

'How?'

'I could give him a story, one with all the elements he likes, that might push a few of his buttons.'

'How do you mean?' Tristan asked.

'Well, let's look at Lonnie's life so far: he's been ostracized, locked away for fear he'll bring shame on his family, let down at every turn, made feel to different and ashamed of who he is . . . if there was a fantasy story that sort of combined all those elements, it might just open up something for him.'

Tristan rubbed his chin.

'And you propose to write such a story?'

'I'd like to have a go at it, yes.'

'And how will you get him to read it?'

'We're friends now, he and I. I'll just tell him I've written something, and want his opinion on it, what with him being a big reader and all.'

Tristan shrugged. I could tell he was a bit dubious. 'Okay,' he said. 'It can't hurt.'

The following lunchtime, when Lonnie came in, I handed him an A4-size envelope, with some pages inside.

'What's this?'

'I've been doing some writing,' I said. 'I'd like you to read it and give me your honest opinion.'

'What if I hate it?'

'Then say so.'

'I will.'

'I know.'

'What's it called?'

'It's a fantasy story. It's called "The Wolf Boy".'

'Are there any dwarves in it?'

'There are.'

'Is the hero a dwarf?'

'You'll have to read it and see, won't you?'

'I'll read it tonight.'

'I'd appreciate that.'

This is what I wrote:

The Wolf Boy

Part I

Not so very long ago, and not so very far away, there was a great forest that stretched right across the land.

In this forest there lived many different birds: the little robins with their red breasts, the big black crows with their deep voices, the tiny brown wrens with their stubby tails, the night-jars, who made their nests on the ground and came out only after dark, and the skylarks, with their beautiful sweet song. The forest was home to lots of animals too: the red-haired fox with his handsome face, the wise gentle badger, who lived in a great sett under the earth, the spiky hedgehog, all slow and snuffly, the quiet pine marten, who could climb trees just like a squirrel, and the mice, who came and went without a rustle.

In the caves that could be found right in the heart of the great forest lived the dwarves, who mined for gold and silver deep down among the roots and the soil, and took sparkling diamonds and glittering emeralds from the rocks with their picks and shovels. By the river that ran along the western edge of the great forest dwelt the elves, who built boats of ash, kept hives of bees which made the most delicious honey, and tended great gardens of beautiful, sweet-smelling flowers. And in a clearing, under an ancient oak, in a little house with honeysuckle round the windows and doors, lived a little boy called Joseph and his mother and father.

Joseph loved his life in the forest. He knew the names of all the birds, animals and plants, and spent his days playing in the long grass, climbing trees and fishing for brown trout in the clear waters of the Blue River.

Joseph's father was a woodsman. He was friends with the elves, whom he helped by cutting down trees for them to make into their boats. They gave him honey and fresh flowers for the table. The dwarves liked and trusted him, because he brought them logs to burn in their fires (sometimes it got very cold underground). They gave him tools they made with their nimble hands: a sturdy spade or a bright sharp knife.

Joseph's mother was a huntress. She caught wild rabbits and hares for the pot, and this was good for the great forest, because these animals sometimes grew too great in number and ate the young shoots until none were left. She knew all the wild berries that were pleasant to eat, the mushrooms that tasted nice and were safe to put in a stew, and which trees had sweet sap to make toffee.

So the little family lived in great peace and happiness. The forest gave them everything they needed.

One night in winter, there came a knock on the door. Joseph answered it, and there in the snow stood Brownbeard the dwarf.

'Hello, Brownbeard.'

'Hello, young Joseph. I would like to speak to your parents.'

'You had better come in, then.'

'Thank you.'

Joseph's father got Brownbeard some bread and honey and a cup of tea.

'I am here to warn you,' said the dwarf. 'Greyfang has come back to the forest with his pack.'

Joseph had never seen his father look so frightened. His mother went and got her gun from the chest, and placed it by the door.

'Who is Greyfang?' Joseph asked.

'Greyfang is the king of all the wolves in the land,' Brownbeard said. 'He is as tall as a horse, his teeth can bite through a tree trunk, and fire leaps from his eyes. He is a great and terrible wolf, and he is a man-eater.'

'Once, when you were only a baby,' Joseph's mother said as the shadows grew long in the little house, 'I was out shooting ducks on a frozen lake. I had you in a sling on my back. We used to have a hound called Gerret, and he was running out among the reeds and bringing the birds I had shot back to me, when I suddenly heard him whine. It was a noise I had never known him make before. I ran in the direction of the sound, and found Gerret lying on the ground, his throat torn out and a huge, snarling wolf standing over him as he died.

'I knew it was Greyfang, for there was no other wolf of that size in the forest. He made to spring at me, but my gun was loaded, and I shot at him, hitting him in the shoulder. He turned, and fled back into the trees. It is said that he has never forgiven me for wounding him that day. I heard, shortly afterwards, that he had left the forest with his wild pack.'

'At last he has returned,' Brownbeard said. 'I have seen him. Whitemane, our chieftain, asked me to travel across the forest to the dwarf outpost in the north. They have found a rich vein of jewels there, and have called for more miners to join them, the better to take the precious stones from the rocks where they lie. So, yesterday, before the sun had climbed over the top of the trees, I set out to help my cousins.

127

'I walked all through the day and by nightfall I was still a long way from the mouth of the Northen Caves. Dark snow clouds were covering the moon, and Jack Frost was dancing on the branches of the trees all about – it was bitterly cold. I was thinking of making camp for the night, when I heard a commotion, as if many big dogs were fighting over a juicy bone. I followed the sounds, which led me to an open space in the trees. And there I found the wolves.

'I hid behind a bush, downwind, so they could not smell me, and I watched and listened. There were many, many wolves: big males with long shaggy fur; young pups who rolled and played in the thick snow; old females with wrinkled snouts. And in the centre of them all, fighting to the death, was Greyfang and a young male. They bit and tore at one another with their teeth and claws, and as they fought hundreds of yellow eyes watched them and countless voices howled and roared at the night sky. Long they fought, but at last Greyfang caught the young male by the throat, and that was the end of the fight. The clearing fell silent, and Greyfang, the blood of his enemy still dripping from his mouth, spoke to his pack. "Does any other among you wish to best me and take my place as king?" he growled, and there was not a sound from any of them. "I have brought you back to the great forest because it is time we claimed it as our own once more. The dwarves have grown fat and proud, the elves weak and vain. The men who walk under the trees are few, and will be little threat to us. The clearings and valleys are full of fat deer and plump rabbits. We can live here without fear. The great forest will be ours again."

'And then he threw back his big, grey head and howled long and deep, and the sound of it cast a shadow of terror across my heart. I abandoned my visit to the Northern Caves, and made haste back to my people with the news. Whitemane bade me warn you immediately, because it is well known Greyfang bears you no love, Huntress, for the hurt you dealt him.'

Brownbeard finished his tea and said goodnight to Joseph and his family. The child was full of questions about wolves, for he had never seen one. There was not an animal in the forest that he feared. Even the wild boar, with its tusks and trampling hoofs seemed more frightened of him than he was of it. But his father hushed him, and told him it was time for bed. Joseph lay there as the candle burned low, listening to his mother and father whispering long into the night. He could not hear what they were saying, no matter how hard he tried, and as the moon poked its head above the trees outside, he fell asleep.

The next morning, when Joseph awoke, he found his father sitting at the table, reading a note. Joseph's mother was not there, and Joseph thought his father had been crying. That frightened him, because his father never cried.

'Where's my mother?' Joseph asked.

'She has gone hunting the great wolf,' his father said. His voice was very quiet and sad.

'That is good,' Joseph said. 'The others will flee when she kills their king.'

'Go and draw some water to wash with,' his father said in that same small voice.

Joseph did as he was told.

The huntress did not come back that night or the next. Joseph's father sat outside the door of their little house waiting long into the night, but there was no sign of her. A week passed, and every morning Joseph leapt out of his bed to see if she had returned while he was asleep, but his father was always up sitting at the window, gazing out into the trees, fingering the sharp edge of his axe, and still she did not come. Joseph knew she was a great huntress, and that she had beaten Greyfang once before, and he tried to be brave. But he was just a little boy – he had not had his ninth birthday yet – and some nights he missed her so much that he cried himself to sleep.

Two weeks passed, and Joseph's father took to wandering far and wide during the day, seeking news of his wife. When he returned at night, he was often too tired to cook their dinner, so Joseph would cut slices of bread and heat some milk over the fire for them. The woodsman would sit and eat solemnly, his bearskin coat still about his shoulders and his axe at his feet. 'The dwarves have not seen her,' he would say, or, 'No news from the elves,' or, 'The wolves are running. I killed one today.' Then one morning Joseph awoke to find his father gone, and another note on the table.

Joseph was not good at reading, and he had to try many times to read some of the words, and even then he was not sure he understood them all. But he did know what the note meant, even if he could not read every bit of it. This is what the note said:

Dear Joseph,
    I have left to find your mother. I may be gone for some days. There is food enough for you for a week. Stay in the house and do not go outside until I come back. I will find her, I promise.
    I love you, and so does your mother,
    Father

Joseph sat at the table, and cried for a long time. He suddenly felt very lonely.

After a while, he got hungry, and he made himself a sandwich and drank some water. Then he pulled a chair over to the window, and waited for his father and mother to come home.

When it grew dark, Joseph got a little bit afraid. He had never been in the house on his own before, and with all the shadows and the sounds from outside, it seemed to be much bigger and scarier than in the daylight. He tried to light a fire, because it had got very cold, but he had never done that before – his father always lit the fire when he came home from work.

After a while, Joseph gave up, and climbed into bed. He tried very hard not to cry, but he did. He cried until he was too tired to cry any more, and then he fell asleep.

Joesph waited by the window for three whole days, but his parents did not come, so he got out his toys and played with them instead. He looked at the pictures and tried to read the words in the big books his parents kept on the mantelpiece (which they usually would not let him touch). One afternoon, he ate a whole jar of honey with a spoon, and was sick afterwards, and the sick smelt of honey too, but didn't taste nice. Because there was no one to tell him to go to bed, he stayed up as long as he liked; one night, he did not go to bed at all, but pulled some blankets onto the big chair and slept there. He woke up in the cold darkness, with the moon shining in through the window, and heard something snuffling at the front door of the little house.

At first, Joseph thought it was his mother and father returning home. But as he listened, he heard scratching and sniffing, and he realized it was not them – it was an animal. He lay very still, barely breathing. At last, the noise stopped, and he knew that whatever it was had gone. Then, from very close to the clearing where the little house stood, came a long loud howl. Joseph had never heard a wolf howl before, but he knew what the sound was. He pulled the blankets over his head and lay there, shaking with fear, until he felt the first rays of the sun fall warm on his back through the window.

Joseph lost count of the days he lived on his own in the house. One day, he opened the kitchen cupboard and there was no food.

That's okay, he thought. I'm not really very hungry.

But he soon *got* hungry.

Joseph was not a stupid child, and he knew how to find food in the forest. But his father had told him not to leave the house until he returned. So Joseph did not go out to get food.

The next day, Joseph was so hungry he had a pain in his tummy. The day after that, the pain was gone, but he felt too tired to do anything. The following morning, Joseph knew that he had to find food to eat, or he would get very ill. He also knew that something must have happened to his parents.

'I will go to the dwarves. They will help me,' he said.

So he put on his coat and boots, took a sharp, dwarfish knife from the chopping board, and went outside.

The following day, Lonnie marched straight up to me.

'What happens to that kid, Joseph?'

'I'm working on the next chapter. I'll have it for you soon.'

'Write faster.'

'Am I to take it that you liked the story then?'

'When he was left all alone ... you wrote that well. I remember being scared, like that.'

'When your mum and your aunt died?'

'And when I first moved into the house on the mountain. It was scary at night, sometimes.'

'I'll bet it was.'

'In the big house, when I was lonely, I could open up this little window, and stick my head out, and I could smell the air and hear the cars, and there was sometimes the sound of people talking or dogs barking. Then I didn't feel like I was all by myself. But when I moved to the mountain – there was nothing. No streetlamps, no cars, no people ... it was as though I was living in a big black hole, with nobody in it but me.'

I laughed. 'I think there might just be a writer in you, Lonnie Whitmore.'

'Hurry up with chapter two,' he said, and went to hang up his coat.

24

The unit seemed bizarrely quiet without Max. But it seemed positively dead when Annie did not come in on the second day of his sulking absence.

The end of the week arrived, and she was still missing.

'Well, she's a hardy young one, and it's not usual for her to miss days, but it's not unheard of,' Beth Singleton told me. 'There have been one or two days when she got some really nasty bug or other, and couldn't come in. I wouldn't worry yourself about it. She'll be back.'

The weekend came and went, and Annie still did not come in to work. Max returned, however, giving me a wide berth. I was too worried about Annie by then to bother treading back over our row. I had told Sukie about it, and she had given him a good talking to, so I was off the hook, anyway.

'D'you think one of us should go out there?' I asked the gathered staff members at a team meeting that evening. 'Maybe she's really sick and needs a doctor. I wouldn't trust that father of hers to get her medical help if she needed it. He's more likely to call the vet and have her destroyed.'

'William is probably fonder of her than any of us know,' Tristan said. 'He makes sure she is up and ready to come to the unit every day, and pays what money he can for trips and materials. He knows we'd take her and ensure she wants for nothing, but he gives anyway.'

'I saw no love the few times I met him,' I said.

'That's sort of it, though, isn't it?' Beth said. 'You've encountered him, what, twice? It's not really much of an indicator, is it?'

'Well, if she's not here tomorrow, I'm going out there,' I said.

'All right,' Tristan said. 'But more than likely she'll be here, bright and early, with a perfectly reasonable excuse.'

That day, I had been given an illustration of what things had been like with Dominic before his epilepsy had been brought under control. It happened during a role-play exercise. Tristan often introduced issues into the drama module that were perhaps too upsetting to discuss head-on with the group, but which could be handled as a kind of game through acting and pretend.

So, Dominic was pretending to be walking home from the shop, and Tristan was a man in a car, who had stopped and was offering to give him a lift. The problem we were having was that the whole point of the thing was based on the fact that Tristan was supposed to be a stranger, but Dominic could not remember this, and kept on agreeing to get into the car with him.

'Okay,' Tristan said, patiently. 'In the game, you don't know me, Dominic, and I want you to come for a drive. But of course, you should never get into a car with someone you don't know, should you?'

'My daddy bring me home in the car at four o'clock,' Dominic said brightly.

'I know that, Dominic,' Tristan said. 'But that's not for a long time yet. Okay, let's try again. What are you doing?'

'I walkin' home from the shop.'

'Good. And what did you buy?'

Dominic dissolved into giggles.

'What did you buy there, Dominic?'

'Sweets.'

'And what else?'

'A Daniel O'Donnell CD.'

'And what else?'

'A cake for my mammy's tea.'

'Very good. Now, you're walking home, and you're tired and hungry, and a man comes up in his car and stops beside you.'

Tristan made the noises of a car drawing up to the kerb, and mimed pulling up the handbrake.

'Hello, young man,' he said, in a deep voice.

''Lo, Tristan.'

'No, remember, Dominic, you don't know who I am. I'm a stranger.'

'Oh, yeah.'

'So – hello, young man. Could you tell me how to get to the supermarket?'

'Yeah! Supermarket near my house!'

'Well, why don't I give you a lift there, and you can show me?'

'Okay, Tristan.'

The entire room groaned in exasperation – all except Tristan who, without so much as a grimace, went right back to the beginning of the exercise. It was at this point that Dominic suddenly went quite rigid and jerked for a moment. Then his eyes rolled back in his head, and he keeled over backwards with a crash.

Tristan was out of his seat in a moment and kneeling beside him.

'It's okay,' he said – Elaine and some of the others were looking quite alarmed. 'He'll be fine in a minute. No need to get upset.'

A pool of urine began to spread from beneath Dominic. Beth went and got some kitchen towels.

'There's really not a whole lot we can do,' Tristan said. 'He'll come out of it when he's ready. There used to be all this nonsense about people swallowing their tongues, or biting the insides of their mouths during seizures, but there's no record of anything like that ever really happening from what I can tell.

Someone just needs to sit with him and let him know he's okay when he comes around. He'll feel a bit yucky when he does, and will want something warm to drink.'

'I've laid out some clothes for him in the bathroom,' Millie called over.

'Thank you, Millie,' Tristan said.

Suddenly Dominic trembled, and tried to sit up.

'There you go, fella,' Tristan said. 'You're all right.'

'I have a seizure, Tristan?'

'You did.'

Dominic suddenly realized that he had wet himself, and his eyes filled with tears.

'Don't tell my daddy,' he said, clutching at Tristan's arm. 'I a big boy. No wet myself no more.'

'Now now, there's no need for a fuss,' Tristan said, helping Dominic up. 'There was nothing you could have done. It really was an accident, and your daddy won't be at all cross.'

'An accident?'

'That's all.'

'Come on to the bathroom and we'll get you cleaned up,' I said.

He came with me, holding my hand.

'I a big boy, Shane, right?'

'You're bigger than me, that's for sure,' I said.

Dominic giggled. 'Lonnie say you a short-arse hippy.'

'He said that?'

'Yeah,' Dominic giggled. 'He funny.'

'He sure is.'

25

Annie did not come in the next day, so after work, I followed the winding road up Mount Muireann. I parked at the end of the tree-lined laneway, and walked. It was much further than I remembered, and I was hot and thirsty by the time I reached the place where the house jutted out into the path.

'Hello,' I called. 'Anyone about?'

I could not find a door at first. The house just seemed to be a long unbroken stone structure. Finally I reached the end of it, and round the corner I found a low door leading down three steps into a dark dingy room. There was no furniture in it other than an ancient washing machine, with the drum out of it and in pieces on the floor.

'Annie? Mr Kelleher?'

The light behind me was suddenly obscured.

'What d'you want?'

William Kelleher was silhouetted in the doorway.

'Annie hasn't been in to Drumlin in almost a week, Mr Kelleher,' I said, trying not to sound as afraid as I was.

'So?'

'I was worried she might be sick, or that you might need something.'

Slowly, he came down the steps and stood in front of me. I had to crane my neck to speak to him.

'Is she okay?'

'She's fine. Off about the mountain, now, with her cousin.'

'Why hasn't she been in, then?'

'We have visitors. Family over to stay. She loves her cousin Charlie. He understands her. Talks to her. She don't get to play much – be a kid – so I left her off to ramble with him.'

I had not expected that. In the last thirty seconds, this man had said more, and expressed more affection for his daughter, than I had gotten from him during our previous encounters put together.

'I was just going to have a drink,' he said. 'You'll have one with me?'

'Yeah . . . okay, thanks.'

He strode past me and went out of a door in the far wall. I realized this odd, subterranean room was just an entrance hall and followed him. On the other side of the door were more steps, this time going up into a wide living area, the main wall of which had been decorated with a mural of the mountain, complete with a variety of very accurately drawn animals and birds. The furniture was plain and simple, and looked to have been mostly hand-crafted. I sat on a wooden chair with a woollen pillow, and William, who had been rooting in a rough wooden press, came out with a bottle and two glasses, which he set on a low table.

'I made this meself,' he said, pouring some clear liquor into the glasses.

I had a sniff. 'Poteen?'

'Aye. My father made it, and his father before him. You won't find a better drop in these parts.'

I took a sip. It wasn't bad at all. I made a mental note to call a taxi for the home journey. I would be in no state to drive.

'I never thanked you for bringing my girl home from town that night,' William said.

'That was a long time ago, Mr Kelleher.'

'Call me Will, please. You make me feel like I'm in court.'

'Will, then. That seems almost a lifetime ago, now. I was glad to get her home safely.'

'She doesn't run off much. Her ma and me, we'd had a row. She got scairt, and went like a frightened fox.'

'You didn't go after her?'

'No. She always comes back, sooner or later.'

I took out a cigarette and offered him one. He took it, with thanks.

'Some days, I think she's almost normal, nearly right. She'll say somethin' that's almost genius. She's brilliant with the animals, and she can tell you the name of every tree and plant hereabouts. You see that picture on yon wall?'

'I do.'

'She painted that.'

I wondered if Tristan knew Annie was so gifted an artist. He had never mentioned it.

'She can be the sweetest, most devoted daughter a man could wish for. But you know, I can't ask her to boil a kettle to make tea, because she'd scald herself, or set the place alight. She won't dress herself unless her mother stands there and hands her every item of clothes in the right order. She wouldn't eat if food wasn't put in front of her. *I* know she's a beauty, but she doesn't. You have to be so careful of her around lads because she has no idea of what kind of message she can send out. God almighty, it's heartbreaking, sometimes, Shane.'

I hadn't introduced myself and was surprised he knew my name. I supposed Annie had mentioned me.

'But you love her.'

He seemed uncomfortable for a moment. Then he said, 'I have three other children. They have all moved on – they have no love of the land or of this place my family has lived in for generations. This mountain – we once owned most of it. It's important to know where you come from, to appreciate what that has made you. Now, Annie, she adores the house, the fields, the stones. See the mantel.'

The shelving over the enormous fireplace was full of different types of stones and crystals of many different colours, shapes and textures. There were several of the sort Annie had given me on my first day at Drumlin.

'Present for you,' she had said. 'Piece of my home. Piece of my heart.'

I felt my eyes filling up with tears.

'Of course I love her,' William said. 'She's like a part of me.'

I sat back down, rubbing at my eyes so he wouldn't see I'd been crying.

'Pour me some more of that fine poteen,' I said. 'Let's drink to Annie.'

William laughed heartily, and unscrewed the lid.

'Watch yourself with this, now, it packs quite a punch.'

It did. I have only vague memories of getting home.

26

Annie did finally return to Drumlin a week later. Autumn was coming down fast, and her dress was the colour of the leaves that blew and chased one another across the yard outside the unit. In news, she told us about her relatives, who were staying with her family.

'My cousin Charlie. He likes me,' she said. 'Sings songs and plays games. Walks in the trees and the fields and by the rivers and streams. Charlie my friend since we were small.'

'He sounds like a nice visitor to have,' Sukie said. 'How long is he staying?'

'He will be with us until the first day of Christmas,' Annie said, singing the last few words. 'There'll be snow on the ground and frost on the trees before he leaves.'

'You've lots of time with him, in that case,' Tristan said.

'Time, time, time is on my side,' Annie said, rocking back and forth and waving her arms above her head.

I noticed that for the rest of the day she seemed more muted than usual. She took part in everything we did, and if I had not known her, I would have seen nothing different. Yet there was a spark missing – something absent in the way she dealt with everyone, and in how she went about the business of the day. I wrote it off as perhaps being a sign that she was tired. I did not doubt she'd been up late most of the nights she'd been away, or that she was missing Charlie, her cousin.

I have to admit, I wondered about him. William had given me the impression that he was in no way intellectually disabled, but a reasonably average young man, who just happened to have an affinity with his strange, wonderful relative. From listening to what Annie's father had said, and what Annie herself had told us, I had an image of a virtual saint. I was sure he could not possibly be like that, in actuality, and I was certainly intrigued. I could not wait to meet him.

PART 7

Among the Stones

Once upon a time there were three billy goats, who were to go up to the hillside to make themselves fat, and the name of all three was 'Gruff'.

On the way up was a bridge over a cascading stream they had to cross; and under the bridge lived a great ugly troll, with eyes as big as saucers, and a nose as long as a poker, and teeth as sharp as razor blades. He had come up to the hillside to get fat too, but instead of grass, he planned to gorge himself on goat meat, or the flesh of an occasional passing child . . .

From *The Three Billy Goats Gruff*, a traditional
Norwegian folk tale

27

'My daddy picking me up at four. O. Clock,' Dominic said for the twentieth time that morning.

'He is,' I said, pushing the paints over so they were right in front of the huge boy. 'But you should really paint something. It's art time. Messy time.'

Dominic had a sheet tied about his neck so that it didn't matter if he chose to paint himself rather than the paper, but there was not a single blotch or speck upon its white surface.

'Not. Paintin'.' Dominic said, and folded his arms.

I shrugged.

'Okay. I'll just have great fun painting a lovely picture myself, then.'

I tried to apply Tom Sawyer's 'picket fence' approach to the job at hand, but Dominic was too clever for me by far. Each and every time I suggested that this was just about the best fun it was humanly possible to have, he simply snorted and turned his chair away.

'I. Am. Not. Paintin'.'

When the session was finished, I had produced five sheets of brightly coloured paper (my attempts at art tend to be of the Jackson Pollock variety), while Dominic had not so much as generated a single brush stroke.

As we sat around in the group afterwards, admiring one another's handiwork, I noticed that Dominic was beginning to regret his 'not paintin'' stance.

'Oh Ricki, that is a lovely picture,' Beth gushed. 'Tell us all about it.'

It is worth remembering that when someone puts in a great effort to produce a picture, the worst insult you can level is to ask: 'What's that then?' It is far better to simply ask them to explain to you what they have created. I have found that even professional artists appreciate this approach.

'Well, that's my mammy there,' Ricki said, indicating an orange splodge.

'My daddy picking me up at four o'clock,' Dominic said loudly.

'Ricki is telling us about her picture now,' Beth said. 'You decided not to paint today, Dominic, so you will not have a turn telling us about your picture.'

'Paint now!' Dominic said eagerly.

'No, the exercise is over. You'll have to wait until next time. Go on, Ricki.'

'And this is my daddy –'

'I'm. Paintin'. Now,' Dominic said, and swept his chair backwards.

'Sit down, Dominic,' Beth said. 'You had a chance, and you made your decision.'

Dominic ignored her, and walked swiftly to the table where the paints were still laid out. He slammed a fresh page down before him, and took a brush and plunged it into the first pot that came to hand.

'Dominic, sit down this instant!' Beth said.

I stood up, but as I did so, Tristan came in from his office, obviously roused by Beth's raised voice. Dominic froze when he saw him, but his jaw set, and he continued to paint. Tristan did not pause for an instant. He strode across the room, and took Dominic by the arm.

'You know very well, young man, that when the group is together, we join it and participate,' Tristan said firmly. 'Now I would like you to please stop this and sit back down.'

Dominic began to do as he was told, allowing Tristan to lead him out from behind the table, but then, without warning, he turned rapidly, grabbed the table with all the painting para-phernalia still on it, and flung it across the room. Tristan just managed to get out of its trajectory, while paint, brushes, paper and pots of water flew every which way. The table itself clattered to the ground, its legs pointing at the ceiling. The room was thick with silence and tension. I expected Dominic to go on the rampage, and I jumped up to help restrain him, but instead, he continued over to the group and sat in the chair he had vacated.

'Dominic, you will please come with me,' Tristan, who was standing among the detritus in the art area, said. 'I think we need to talk.'

To my utmost surprise, the giant stood and followed Tristan out of the room.

'Now, Ricki,' Beth said, 'back to your painting.'

Twenty minutes later, Tristan and a red-eyed Dominic came back out to the workroom.

'Excuse me, everyone,' Tristan said. 'Dominic has thought long and hard about what happened during group. He's done some tough work with me about it, and he's got something he'd like to say.'

Dominic, who was standing with his head lowered said, so quietly we all had to strain to hear it, 'I sorry for what I done. Hurt your feelings. Hurt my feelings.'

Ricki tentatively came over, and looked up at him.

'That's all right, Dominic,' she said. 'We all get cross from time to time.'

He looked at the tiny woman, and said in a voice full of tears, 'I sorry, Ricki. You my friend?'

'Of course I am, Dominic.'

Bending almost double, Dominic reached down, and gave her a hug that must have caused her ribs to pop.

'Okay, let's go back to work,' Tristan said.

And without further comment, everyone did.

The Wolf Boy

Part II

Joseph had been to see the dwarves many times, and he knew the way to their underground kingdom well. As he walked, he spied some old apples that had not yet fallen, high in the branches of a tree. He knew they would be hard and sour, but he was very hungry, so he climbed up and picked them. Further on, he found a patch of wild garlic and a bush heavy with hazelnuts. He ate these too, then broke the ice on a little pond and took a long drink. As he was bending over the water, he heard a low growl. Slowly, he raised his head, and there, looking down on him, was an enormous grey wolf.

'You should not be out on such a cold day, manchild,' said the wolf. Its voice was low and hoarse, as if it had been shouting a lot. 'Where are your parents?'

'My mother went out to hunt Greyfang, king of the wolves, many days ago,' Joseph said, for he knew well that it was to Greyfang himself he was speaking. 'When she did not return, my father went in search of her. I dare say they are near and will fall upon you any second. They will kill you and we shall make a fine rug out of your hide.'

The wolf shook its massive hairy head, and its tongue lolled out, as if to taste the freezing air.

'I fear, manchild, that you are mistaken. Your mother, I am sorry to say, shot me five years ago not far from here. She came hunting me, as I was hunting her, three weeks past. We met in the great cedar groves by the Purple Coach Road, and I killed her there before she could even raise her gun. Your father looked for me with his axe, but my guards stopped him before he reached our camp to the south. He cut the heads off three before he was taken down, but he, too, is dead.'

Joseph felt the sting of tears, but also a great and terrible anger. Greyfang watched him with huge brown eyes, and saw the rage that was building within the boy.

'Well, wolf,' Joseph said, clutching the knife in his pocket. 'If you have slain my mother and father, then I am bound to kill you.'

Greyfang did not laugh, for he saw that the boy meant every word. 'I cannot fight you, child. You are not yet a man, and I am old among my kind. Go in peace and wait for the years to add to your size and strength. If you still wish it then, we can do battle.'

'I stand before you now, wolf!' Joseph shouted, tears streaming down his cheeks.

'I have sharp teeth and jagged claws, child,' said Greyfang. 'You have only soft flesh and a plump heart. I would kill you surely.'

'Then so be it,' said Joseph. 'But I will cause you great hurt before you are done with me.'

'Very well,' said the wolf, 'though it saddens me to kill a pup.'

And with a roar, Greyfang sprang across the pond in a single leap. Joseph was ready, and just as the wolf was upon him, the boy pulled out his knife. Yelping in pain, Greyfang rolled away, the knife's blade stuck deep in his grey fur.

'You have claws after all, manchild,' the wolf said, lying in the snow, panting like a huge dog. 'You have wounded me.'

Just then, Joseph heard barking, and out of the trees scampered three small wolf cubs. 'Father, Father, why are you bleeding?' they called as they ran to Greyfang, nestling against his flanks.

'This hunter has left his mark upon me, children,' said Greyfang, looking at Joseph.

Joseph saw the cubs gaze at him in fear, and then look with worry at their father. He did not feel like a brave hunter at all, but more like a boy who has had very little to eat and has just learned that he is an orphan. He sat in the snow feeling sick and tired and very, very sad.

'Are you going to kill us?' one of the cubs asked him.

Joseph shook his head. 'I am not a hunter,' he said. 'I am just a boy.'

Shakily, Greyfang stood up, and as he did so, the knife fell from his side. 'Take your claw, manchild,' he said. 'You may have need of it in the future.'

With the cubs at his heels, the great wolf turned away from Joseph and disappeared into the darkness beneath the trees.

The dwarves were surprised to see Joseph arrive at the door to their cave town all alone as night was falling, but they brought him in and sat him by the fire and gave him meat soup thickened with biscuit crumbs. Sitting about the great hall, they listened as he told the story of how his mother and then his father had left him to hunt Greyfang and his kind, and of how he had met and fought the wolf and pierced him. The dwarves, who were far more sensitive than they looked, mopped at their tears with their beards when they heard the news of the deaths of the woodsman and huntress. Whitemane, the old chief, sat Joseph at his feet, and placed his thick-fingered hand on his shoulder. 'Tomorrow, we shall ride out on our ponies and we will hunt every last one of these wolves until the forest is rid of them,' he said. 'You may ride at my side, and have your revenge.'

The next day an army of dwarves rode out of the caves, dressed in armour fashioned from iron and carrying axes and swords. Joseph sat on a sturdy brown pony and rode beside Whitemane and his son, Redlocks. 'We will bring a cartload of wolf heads back to the caves tonight, my boys,' Whitemane said, laughing as they rode through the trees.

They had not gone far when there arose about them the sound of many wolves howling. The voices of the beasts drifted through the winter air and came from every direction. The horses started to whinny in fear. They did not like the song of the wolves at all. The dwarves muttered and placed their hands on their weapons.

Joseph did not even see the first wolf leaping from the cover of the trees, but before he knew it, grey shapes were springing upon the dwarves and knocking them from their horses everywhere he looked. The dwarves fought bravely, but there were too many wolves, and it was not long before most of the dwarves were either dead or dying. Joseph was too frightened to move. The brown pony neighed and tried to run this way and that, but everywhere it turned there was a wolf snapping at its hooves. Finally, the little horse reared, and Joseph was thrown from the saddle onto the cold, hard ground. He hit his head on the stump of a tree, and everything went black.

When Joseph finally awoke, the first thing he saw was the night sky, with thousands of stars winking in the blackness. He found he could not move, but he was warm and comfortable. It took him a few moments to realize that he was lying amid a great bundle of sleeping wolf cubs, who lay atop and over him just like a blanket. He craned his neck, and was just about able to see a vast gathering of wolves in a clearing a little way off. Greyfang was in the centre of them, and he was addressing the group. Joseph could catch only the odd word, but this is what the wolves were saying.

'I say we kill him,' an old male snarled.

'We kill for food, Silverbrow,' Greyfang said. 'You have eaten well today. I'd say the taste of dwarf blood is still on your tongue. What reason is there to slay the manchild? He is no threat to us.'

'He brought the miners,' a female said.

'The dwarf men rode out because I slew the manchild's parents, who were their friends,' Greyfang said. 'The huntress came to kill me, for that was her way. It was said by the forest folk that I bore her ill-will, and she wished to slay me before I did the same to her. I had no choice, in the end, though I tried to tell her I had no desire for her blood.'

'How did this argument begin?' Silverbrow asked.

'I was out hunting fowl once, many years ago, when a large hound fell upon me. I had one of my sons from that season's litter along to learn hunting skills, and I had to kill the dog, for fear it would take my pup. The huntress found us just as the hound died, and put a bullet in my shoulder. I fled, but she always believed I would return for revenge upon her.'

'You promised us peace!'

'You swore we would be free!'

'You spoke of fat, idle dwarves and frightened men!'

There was a great uproar among the wolves then, and Greyfang had to shout to be heard over them. 'I tried to find the woman, to tell her I wanted peace. She would not believe me. Humans think we are vicious and evil, and nothing I can say would change that.'

'Her mate came too,' a young male shouted, coming right up to Greyfang, his teeth bared and hair standing on end all down his back. 'He killed my brother Darkfur with his axe.'

'Yes, Blackpaw, and you in turn killed him.'

'I want the child!' Blackpaw roared, and made as if to leap at Greyfang. The great wolf reached out one of his huge paws, and knocked the youngster aside as if he were a fly.

'None of you will touch the manchild, for he is here under my protection,' Greyfang said.

A slender, fair-haired female wolf stepped up beside Greyfang.

'I am Goldcrest, Greyfang's mate,' she said.

The pack fell silent, for Goldcrest was known as gentle and kind, and was well loved. 'This child, who never lifted a paw against us, has been sorely wronged. He is alone in the world, adrift in the cold woods without guidance. My husband and I request that he be given the shelter of the pack.'

There was complete silence, then a great explosion of snarls, barks, yelps and howls, as the gathering of wolves all tried to speak at once.

'A human in the pack? It is unheard of!'

'He could never run with us. He has only two legs, and they are short.'

'He is bald and pink, and his teeth are blunt and useless.'

While all this had been happening, Joseph had been struggling to escape from the bundle of wolf cubs. By pulling this way and that, wriggling and squirming, he finally got one arm out, and gradually, a little at a time, pulled himself upright. On his tiptoes, he crept through the trees until he was just outside the circle of wolves and could hear what they were saying.

You must remember, this was a very hard time for Joseph. He was lost and alone out in the forest at wintertime. He had just found out that his parents were dead, and now he had been captured by the very creatures who had killed them. He was afraid, but angry too. Then he heard what Greyfang said about his mother and father, and he was confused.

If Greyfang had really been looking for his mother to try and make friends, and had only killed her defending himself, that meant it wasn't really his fault. And if the other wolves had only killed his father because he had killed some of them, then that wasn't their fault either. And now, Greyfang and his wife were asking the pack to look after Joseph, because they felt badly about what had happened. Joseph listened as the wolves began to say nasty things about him, and he got angry all over again. How dare they say he had short legs! And he certainly was not useless! Without thinking about it, he suddenly stepped out into the clearing among them, his knife in his hand and a fierce look on his face.

The noise of the wolves roaring and snarling got even louder and fiercer, and three of the animals sprang for him at the same time. So quickly that Joseph did not even see him move, Greyfang was in front of the little boy, and two of the wolves were knocked aside by his great paws. The third landed behind Joseph, who turned to meet it. The wolf was too afraid of the sparkling dwarf knife to go any further, and there was also the sight of Greyfang, who now stood beside Joseph, his teeth bared.

153

'I will fight any one of you,' Joseph said as loudly as he could. 'I am not afraid!'

Greyfang placed a paw on Joseph's shoulder, Goldcrest placed her smaller paw on his head, and all the wolves fell back.

'You are a brave one, Joseph,' Greyfang said. Then, to the pack: 'I take this manchild as my son. Any one of you who harms a hair on him, I will kill. From this moment onwards, he is wolf.'

Then Greyfang threw his huge head back and howled, and Goldcrest raised her voice and joined him, and one by one the other wolves added their songs until the night air was filled with their sad, beautiful music.

So Joseph came to live with the wolves. For the first weeks he was always frightened, and barely slept at night. He was sure one of them would creep up on him and swallow him whole as he was asleep. But as the days passed, he came to understand that he was safe. Greyfang and Goldcrest treated him with great tenderness, and their cubs called him brother. That winter, they stayed deep in the forest, and were undisturbed by man, dwarf or elf. Joseph missed his mother and father terribly, and would often walk off into the trees by himself, feeling sad and lonely. But when he came back to the clearing where the wolves lived, one of his cub brothers would call him to play, and he would find that the bad feelings could be forgotten, for a while at least.

Greyfang loved the forest, and in the first days of spring, he took Joseph and the cubs to many different, special places.

They climbed to the top of Black Mountain, which stood right at the centre of the woods, where Greyfang told them of the golden eagles who had once reigned there.

'I have never seen an eagle,' Joseph said.

'That is because the elves hunted them, to take their feathers to make flights for their arrows,' Greyfang said. 'The eagles do not dwell in the forest any more.'

They walked the length of the Blue River, and Greyfang told

them of the busy beavers, who once built fine dams all along the river's course.

'They sound like funny animals, with their flat tails and bushy whiskers,' laughed Dapplecoat, Joseph's favourite cub brother, 'I hope we see one soon!'

'You will see no beavers, my son,' Greyfang sighed. 'The dwarves hunted them for their hide, to make boots and coats. The beavers no longer dwell in the forest.'

They roamed across the green hills, and Greyfang showed them the shallow, shadowy caves where the gentle black bears would sleep away the cold winters.

'There was nothing prettier than seeing a mother bear playing with her cubs in the early morning sunshine.' Goldcrest smiled at the memory, for she had accompanied them on this trip.

'I would love to play with them,' Joseph said. 'Where are they now?'

'The last of the black bears was shot long before you were born,' Greyfang told him, 'by a huntress.'

Joseph felt a deep pain in his heart when he heard this. 'Not my mother,' he said.

'No, but one much like her,' Greyfang said, and Joseph asked no more questions that day.

Summer came, and the pack moved from their clearing to the northern edge of the forest, where the trees were thinner and herds of deer ran among them, swift as swallows. The wolves hunted what they needed to eat, and left the rest. Joseph did not like the raw meat they ate, but there were plenty of other things for him to live on: nuts and fruit and wild herbs and berries, and though he was sometimes hungry, it never lasted long. The forest always gave him something sooner or later.

One day Joseph was playing with Dapplecoat in a wide meadow, when the cub sat up and said, 'I smell something funny.'

Joseph was always amazed by the things the wolves could smell which he could not. 'I smell nothing, brother,' he said. 'What does it smell like?'

'It smells like you, but stronger and hairier,' Dapplecoat said.

All of a sudden, there was a whizzing noise, and an arrow stuck into Dapplecoat's side. The cub cried out and then lay still, panting hard. Joseph heard the sound of heavy footsteps, and turning, saw a big, dirty-looking man with mud-coloured hair and a thick beard, running towards them through the long grass.

'Do not worry, brother,' Joseph whispered. 'He will hurt you no more.'

Joseph lay down flat on the ground beside Dapplecoat, and waited, hardly breathing. He closed his eyes tight, pretending to be dead, and after a few moments, heard the big man stomping up to them. Even though he was not a wolf, Joseph could smell the hunter now. He smelt of sweat, tobacco and fried bacon, and the stench of him made Joseph feel a little bit ill. Joseph heard him stop, and then grunt in surprise. The man had shot a wolf, but he had not expected to see a little boy there too.

The awful smell got stronger and stronger as the man knelt down to look more closely at Joseph, to see where he was hurt. When he did, Joseph stuck the knife he was holding, hidden at his side, into the big man's arm. The man shouted in pain. Joseph stood up and roared just like Greyfang, jumping up and down and waving his arms. The man shouted again, dropped his bow, and ran away, screaming in a funny high voice.

Dapplecoat had stopped panting, and there was a lot of blood coming out of the wound where the arrow was sticking. Joseph bent down close to his ear, and whispered, 'Hold on, brother. I will get Father. I will run as fast as I can, and bring him to you. He will know what to do.'

The boy found Greyfang drinking from a little stream not far from the meadow, and through his tears told him what had happened.

'Get on my back, Joseph, for I am going to run and you will not keep up with me,' the great wolf growled, and Joseph did as he was told. Greyfang sprang forward, and the wind whooshed into Joseph's face, and the trees whizzed past, and it felt for all the world as if he was flying. 'Hold on tight, my son,' Greyfang said, and Joseph wrapped his arms round the wolf's neck, and laid his face against the fur of his back, and hoped his brother would be all right.

Dapplecoat looked very small and he was lying very still. Greyfang licked the arrow, and gripped it in his teeth, but it would not come out. He nudged the little cub, but Dapplecoat did not whimper or move.

'Can you make him well again, Father?' Joseph asked, his voice shaking.

'No, child,' Greyfang said. 'He is dead.'

That night, Greyfang spoke to the pack.

'I was wrong to bring you here,' he said. 'The great forest is not safe. We will never be at peace here, for there will always be hunters with arrows or guns or swords. Elves, dwarves or men, they are all the same. I can lead you no more. I am going into the mountains, where no men walk.' He looked at Joseph. 'My son, it is a hard place to which I take Goldcrest and my litter. There will be no trees with nuts, no bushes with berries. The wind always blows and the sun rarely shines. I do not think you can follow.'

'The caves where the dwarf miners tunnel are not far from here,' Goldcrest said. 'I will take you there.'

'But I am not a dwarf,' Joseph said, his eyes filling with tears.

'Nor are you a wolf,' Greyfang said, and he would not look at Joseph, or listen to his arguments.

28

Hallowe'en came, and with it the first really cold weather we'd had all year.

I was working with Dominic on a costume for our Hallowe'en party. He was to be Frankenstein's monster, and a very fine one he would have been, too, had he not kept bursting into uncontrollable fits of giggles every time he saw his reflection.

'I. Am. A. Monster,' he declared every thirty seconds. 'Shane, I'm going to scare my mammy.'

'Dom, you'll scare absolutely everyone,' I said. 'In fact, I'm really scared right now.'

'You scared o' me, Shane?' Dominic asked, sounding a bit unsure if this was a good thing or not.

'It's a nice kind of scared,' I told him. 'Like when you go on a roller-coaster.'

We continued working. I was trying to find a way to attach the bolts to Dominic's muscular neck, when he blurted out:

'I love Sukie, Shane.'

'Yeah, she's a lovely girl, all right.'

'Yeah.'

There was a pause.

'Sukie my girlfriend.'

'I don't think so, Dominic,' I said.

'She is. I gonna dance with her at the party, so I am.'

'Good for you. Sure we'll all have a dance, won't we?'

'Yeah.'

We worked on for a few moments.

'I. Loves. Sukie.'

'Doesn't everyone?' I said.

'Yeah.'

I thought no more about what Dominic had said until it was too late.

29

No Hallowe'en party is complete without ghost stories.

Even though it was the middle of the afternoon, we closed over the window curtains, lit a candle in the centre of the group, and played some eerie music on the stereo. Pumpkins had been carved in a variety of horrifying faces (actually, many of them looked simply smiley), and pictures of ghosts, ghouls, witches and monsters had been put up all over the walls.

We had all sorts of stories, most of the of the well-worn type (Elaine did the old 'and the police told her that the threatening phone calls were coming from within the house' story), and some fairly surreal (Glen decided to act out for us his own version of *Jaws*, which had to be seen to be believed).

Annie waited her turn quietly. Her mood had remained subdued in the weeks since her absence, but we all passed it off as being down to the changed dynamic of the Kelleher homestead.

'It's a princess, and she lives in a lovely house on a beautiful mountain,' Annie began.

'I like princesses,' Sukie said.

'The mountain her friend. The trees she would climb, and the streams play in, and the wind sang songs in her ear all the days. But the princess lonely. Sad, sometimes.'

'Poor girl,' Elaine said.

'She needs magic pots and kettles and candlesticks to be her friends,' Sukie said.

'Or dwarves,' Lonnie said. 'Dwarves make good friends for princesses.'

'Yeah, they don't take up much room, and you can balance a board on their heads and use them as a coffee table,' I said.

'Have you ever read any fairy stories about guitar-playing hippies?' Lonnie shot back. 'No? That's because no one would be even vaguely interested in a story like that.'

'Princess wait for someone to come and stay with her,' Annie continued. 'Make her life happy.'

'I bet it'll be a handsome prince,' Elaine said.

'Or a dwarf,' Lonnie said.

'Or a hippy,' I said.

'Or a magic teapot,' Sukie said.

'She say prayers: "Please dear God, make me so I am same as people, so I can go and be like them in the town. If I could play with the girls in the school, I would not want to hear the singing of the stones or the talk of the pine marten in the trees." And then one day, God answered her.'

'Excuse me, please,' Glen said. 'But is there a ghost, or a monster, or a deranged killer in this story anywhere? Because I'm starting to get bored.'

'Think of it as being a fairytale version of *The Love Boat*,' Beth suggested.

'Will there be celebrity cameo appearances from superstars of the seventies, then?' Glen said, sounding as if he did not hold out much hope that there would be.

'Prince come,' Annie said. 'Princess love him. He talk to her, and he laugh with her, and she think he a great fella.'

'I see true love's kiss coming,' Sukie said.

'Then, one day, while they up on the highest part of the mountains, he take a knife, and he stick it in her.'

'That's more like it,' Glen said. 'Nice one, Annie. I didn't see that coming. I love a shock ending.'

'He stick it in her heart. He stick it in her private places. He stick it in her eyes and in her face.'

'I think that's enough, Annie,' Tristan said, laughing. 'We get the message.'

'Hurt her,' Annie said, her voice petering out to a bare murmur. 'Hurt her deep inside. Broke her heart, yes.'

As she finished, Annie, who had been trembling slightly, seemed to relax and go back in upon herself. But there was something in the way she sat, and looked at her feet, and seemed suddenly much smaller that made me feel uneasy. I began to feel that the subtle change in Annie was more than just about a few more round the table for dinner of an evening.

Something was wrong.

30

After work that day a few of us went out for drinks. The day's festivities had gone off without a hitch; everyone had had a grand time and, after the bus had gone, we convened to a nearby bar.

By the end of the night, there was only myself, Beth and Millie left, and Millie had more than slightly over-indulged, and was dozing, her head against my shoulder.

'Beth, you're a really good care worker,' I told her, at that stage one gets to when just the right amount of alcohol has been consumed, and the world is a wonderful place to be and everyone is your best friend. 'I don't think you get the credit you deserve, though. I mean, if it wasn't for you, there wouldn't be any Drumlin Ther'peutic Place at all, would there? Half the lads were your clients originally, weren't they?'

'Yeah – they were, I s'pose.'

'So how come your name isn't over the door same as Tristan's is? I think you d'serve more respect. I really do.'

'No, you're wrong. I get respec'.'

'From who?'

'You respec' me, dontcha?'

'I do, I do, I think you're great.'

'Tristan respects me.'

'Does he?'

'Course he does.'

I made an exaggerated shrugging motion. 'Where is he?'

'He always goes home early. Early to bed, early to rise, tha's what he says.'

'And when he was goin' he s'gested you should go home, too. Wha's that about?'

'Ah, he always fusses over me. It's how he shows he cares.'

'No, no, I don' agree with that,' I countered. 'It's controlling is what it is. It's none of his fucking business what you do. You're your own woman, Beth. You don' have to do wha' he says.'

'But he's my best friend. He . . . he loves me, and that's why he fusses like he does.'

I drained my glass. The barman had just called time, and I motioned for one last round. I was going to have quite a sore head in the morning, and I might as well be hung for a sheep as a lamb.

'He loves you?'

'Yeah. Like a friend.'

'And you love him?'

'Yeah, but not like you think.'

I waited while our drinks were placed in front of us, and my change counted out.

'Beth, can I have permission to speak candidly?'

She patted me on the shoulder. 'Speak away.'

'Okay, I will. Thank you.'

'You're welcome.'

'See, Beth, I heard a *rumour*.'

'Did you?'

'Yes. I did. A rumour relating to your relationship with Tristan.'

'And what did this rumour suggest?'

'Well, apparently, you and Tristan, at one stage, were more than just good friends.'

'Really?'

'Yes. Now, I am not one to repeat idle gossip.'

'But you just did.'

That stumped me.

'You're right. I'm as bad as anyone else. So, come on, let's hear it. Did you and Tristan do the dirty?'

Beth feigned offence. 'That's not a question you should really ask a lady, now is it?'

'Well, I have a very important motivation for broaching such a sensitive issue.'

'You do?'

'Yeah.'

'What's that?'

'I am absolutely dying to know.'

She broke down laughing at that, and so did I. Millie woke up momentarily, scowled at us, and went straight back to sleep. Finally, we both recovered our composure.

'Okay, I'll tell you the truth,' Beth said. 'Tristan and I did have an affair.'

Now that it was out, I wasn't sure what to say.

'Um . . . okay. Good for you. Sort of.'

'It's not something I'm proud of that I hurt Heddie, who had been, and continues to be, very good to me,' Beth continued. 'But I am not ashamed that I fell in love with Tristan, or he with me. When it happened, it was a lonely time in both of our lives. My husband had just left me, and I was very raw from it. Heddie had just taken a job in the city as a broker, and she was working horrendous hours. Tristan was volunteering at the centre, simply because we had no money to pay him, and he was working that smallholding they had, and I think he was feeling very lost and emasculated.'

'I suppose he went from being the boss in his previous life to being second fiddle,' I observed. 'That can't have been easy.'

'I knew I was attracted to him right away. He's a fine figure of a man, and he just swept into the centre and more or less turned everything on its head. He didn't wait to be asked to tackle Max – he just did it, and within a matter of weeks we could see an improvement. It was the same with Dominic; he just made things better.'

'And how did Heddie find out?'

Beth looked into what was left of her drink, and did not answer.

'If this is too difficult, we can stop,' I said. 'I don't want to put a downer on the night. We've had a good time, and the drink made me stupid.'

'I told Heddie,' she said.

'You told her?' I said, mildly incredulous. I had met Heddie on quite a few occasions, and found her more than a little scary. 'Whatever for?'

'I was staying over at their home very often. I was eating meals at their house regularly, and would be there when she got in at night. This could be eleven or twelve, and Tristan would have long gone to bed. Heddie just wanted to wind down, chat about her day. We became friends. One night I thought: "Two hours ago, I was making love to this woman's husband." And I couldn't keep up the pretence any more. I think there was a large part of me that wanted just to tell *somebody* too.'

'What did she say?'

'Nothing for what felt like a lifetime. She just stared at me. Then she said: "I want you to promise that you will never sleep with him again."'

'Did you?'

'I did. She said that, if we swore to keep things platonic, she would permit us to remain friends and colleagues. She said she'd know if there was anything more going on.'

'And you kept your promise?'

'Yes. Oh, I love him. More than I could ever say. More than I ever loved my husband. But what we have is ... enough.'

'And did Tristan have any say in this?'

'I think that he realized that he'd been given a chance most men never get. He'd strayed, and not only been given another chance, but forgiven. His marriage got a second chance, and he was allowed get on with the life he was making for himself. We never, ever discussed it, but I'd guess he was more than happy with the arrangement.'

'I'll bet he was. And you still stay at their home regularly and see Heddie socially?'

'Yes. We're still friends.'

'Even though she knows you screwed her husband?'

'Even though she knows I still want to.'

PART 8

Last Night I Dreamt That Somebody Loved Me

On the blue summer evenings, I shall go down the paths,
Getting pricked by the corn, crushing the short grass:
In a dream I shall feel its coolness on my feet.
I shall let the wind bathe my bare head.

I shall not speak, I shall think about nothing:
But endless love will mount in my soul;
And I shall travel far, very far, like a gipsy,
Through the countryside – as happy as if I were with a woman.

'Sensation' by Arthur Rimbaud

31

Shortly after Hallowe'en, it was Max's birthday, which of course meant another party. Max's family had agreed to bring him to the unit a little bit later than usual to give us time to put up decorations and to lay out the party food, and we were almost ready when Ricki noticed a glaring omission.

'Where's the rice-crispie buns?'

I set down a plate of egg-mayonnaise sandwiches (Max's favourite) and looked at the assembled spread.

'Umm, it looks like we don't have any, Ricki, but I don't think anyone will miss them. I mean, look at this lot. A feast fit for a king.'

Ricki shook her head. 'We have to have rice-crispie buns. It's a Drumlin tradition. Max will be really disappointed.'

'Come on, Ricki,' I protested. 'There is just about every possible kind of party food here! How could he get in huff over a few measly buns?'

Tristan came over, carrying a tray of plastic cups.

'There's no crispie buns,' Ricki informed him.

Tristan stopped and looked the table over.

'Oh dear,' he said. 'However did that happen?'

'But look at everything else!' I said. 'Surely it's not that important.'

'Shane, crispie buns are the cornerstone of every birthday party,' Tristan said. 'We'll just have to get some before Max comes in.'

'They sell them in the supermarket in town,' Ricki said. 'I seen them the other day.'

'Can you run in and get a batch?' Tristan asked me.

'I'm goin' too,' Dominic, who had just come over to see what all the fuss was about, said.

'That's fine, Dom,' I said. 'Let's go. Max will be here in half an hour.'

The supermarket wasn't too busy on a mid-week morning, and I made straight for the bakery section with Dominic in tow. This proved fruitless, however. No crispie buns were to be found. At Drumlin, everything we did was encouraged to be a learning experience, so I figured this was no different.

'Dominic, you start at this end, and I'll start at the other,' I said. 'If you find the crispie buns, you stay right there until I find you, okay? And I'll do the same until you find me. Understand?'

'Yeah,' Dominic said, and off he went.

I went through row after row of shelves quickly but carefully, and could still not find the desired items. Swearing, and trying to remember if there was a proper bakery store nearby that might just specialize in such a mundane confection, I rounded a corner and came upon Dominic talking to a teenaged girl in the uniform of one of the shop assistants. I saw that he had three packets of what looked to be crispie buns stacked in his arms (Thank God! I thought), but there was something about the girl's body language that gave me pause.

Perhaps I am far too innocent for my own good, but it took me several long moments to work out what I was looking at: the girl was flirting outrageously with Dominic. He, for his part, was beaming from ear to ear, as if all his Christmases had come at once.

'Well, you're a big fella for sure, aren't you?' she was saying, placing her hand on his shoulder. 'I bet you can really handle yourself.'

'Yeah!' Dominic said, giggling with delight.

'You've got a lovely laugh,' his admirer said. 'I bet you've a great sense of humour.'

'Yeah,' Dominic agreed once more, giggling even more hysterically.

I was about to go over and extricate the poor girl from the mess she had placed herself in when Dominic did it for me.

'My daddy pickin' me up at four o'clock,' he said with great seriousness.

'Is he ... ?' the girl said, suddenly beginning to wonder if this guy was quite the find she had thought.

I took the opportunity to intercede.

'I see you got the buns, Dom,' I said, taking his arm.

'Her think I am big. And. Strong,' Dominic said, giggling. 'Her think I a fine thing.'

The poor girl was blushing the same colour as a jar of pickled beetroot.

'Come on, Dominic,' I said, leading him away. 'We have a birthday party to attend.'

'Her like me,' Dominic continued to tell me as we drove back to Drumlin.

'I know, Dominic,' I said.

'My daddy pickin' me up at four o'clock,' he added.

'I know that too,' I said.

The Wolf Boy

Part III

And so it was that a dwarf boy, coming back to the caves early the next morning with a basket of wild strawberries, found a thin, long-haired child asleep on the doorstep. The dwarves did not quite know what to do with this strange creature, and he would not speak to them. He sat in the corner, his hands over his head, and rocked on his heels. It was only when he took the knife from his pocket and attacked them with it, and Yellowhammer, a dwarf warrior, wrestled it from him (receiving a nasty bite for his troubles), that they realized who he was, for the dwarves had inscribed the blade with the names of Joseph's parents, as was their custom when giving such things as gifts.

'It cannot be the huntress's boy,' they said. 'He was slain with the chieftain and his men!'

'There is no other answer to the riddle,' Yellowhammer said. 'This wild boy is Joseph.'

Joseph remained silent and dark-eyed. The kindly dwarves tried to make friends with him. Brownbeard, who had been wounded when the wolves attacked the hunting party so many months before, but had survived, was sent for, but Joseph pretended not to know him. He would not eat the soup or the roasted meats or the bread and honey they put before him, and it was many days before they thought to give him nuts and fresh fruit from the woods. Weeks, and then months went by, and as the time passed the dwarves' patience grew thin. 'Mad Joseph' they called him, and took to ignoring him. He roamed the tunnels and caves beneath the earth, finding places they did not go, and there found peace in the silent dark.

Joseph did not know it, but more than a year had passed when one night he found a narrow passageway down which he had never gone before. He had taken to running on all fours, because it was easier beneath the earth, and because it made him feel more like a wolf. He scurried down this new tunnel, and after a while, felt the breath of fresh air on his face. This breeze was like a drink of water to a man dying of thirst, for with it came the scent of leaves and grass and tree bark. Joseph had forgotten these things after so long hiding in the darkness of the tunnels and living with the blackness that had settled over his heart, and he began to run towards them.

As he ran he took deep breaths, drinking down that beautiful, delicious air. The passageway started to slope upwards, and suddenly, at the end of it he could see a light – a pale silvery light.

Joseph crept out of a narrow opening, and found himself in his beloved forest, many miles away from the Northern Caves. It was night, and a full moon was high in the sky above the trees. From very far away, Joseph heard a long mournful howl. Throwing back his head, he howled back as loudly as he could. After a moment, the other wolf, many miles away, howled in return.

Slowly, but with great joy growing in his soul, Joseph began to walk in the direction of the distant cry.

A rabbit, who happened to be passing on the way to his warren, saw Joseph, walking on all fours, tears streaming down his thin, dirt-smeared cheeks, saying quietly to himself, 'I am coming, Father, I am coming.' The rabbit stopped and watched as the child disappeared into the trees, and then hurried home, wondering who the sad creature had been. And when he got back to his burrow, he held his children tight, and was glad they were all safe and cared for.

And Joseph, the Wild Boy, son of the woodsman and huntress, cub son of Greyfang and Goldcrest, was never seen in the forest again.

32

'What does it mean?' Lonnie asked me.

We were sitting in his living room. The curtains were open, and the mid-morning sun shone through. He had decorated the room with sprigs of holly and heather from the surrounding mountains, and the room smelt of fresh air and rustic life. A small fire was glowing in the hearth, and the room was warm and pleasant.

'What do you think it means?' I said.

'It's a strange, sad story. Does he find Greyfang and Goldcrest?'

'I don't know.'

'You wrote the bloody thing.'

'I know I did. But there are very few absolutes or definites in the world, are there? Sometimes, whether we like it or not, bad stuff happens. Joseph is like any child or little person, and I don't mean that in terms of dwarfism; the dwarves in the story are not little people. I mean he is someone who does not have control over his own life. He is at the mercy of those around him.'

'No one treated him very well,' Lonnie agreed.

'No.'

'But they were all, in their way, well-meaning.'

I thought about that.

'Were they?'

'Yes. His parents went out to hunt Greyfang because they thought he was a threat to their home and their son. The dwarves hunted the wolves for much the same reason. Greyfang and Goldcrest wanted to look after Joseph, because they felt guilty about orphaning him, and they gave him back to the dwarves when they felt they couldn't keep him safe any more. The dwarves tried to care for him, but he wouldn't let them. Everyone wanted what was best ... it all just went wrong, somehow.'

'Is that they way life can be sometimes?'

Lonnie got up and went to the window.

'D'you want to go for a walk?'

He had never asked me that before.

'I'd love to. Sure you're up to it?'

'Yeah. I've been going out a little bit lately. Who did you think picked the heather and the berries?'

'Aisling, I had thought.'

'No. It was me. Come on.'

He put an oversized fedora on his head, and his funny cape-coat, and led me down the lane outside his house. I lit a cigarette.

'So did you like the story in the end?'

'I don't know,' he said. 'It made me feel odd.'

'How?'

'Even though there were dwarves in it, I couldn't identify with them.'

'Oh.'

A blackbird broke cover in front of us and flew loudly from one side of the road to another.

'It was Joseph I could see myself in.'

'He was the hero, I suppose,' I said. 'You're bound to feel sympathetic towards him.'

The pathway slanted gradually upwards as we ascended the mountain. On our left was a low hillock upon which three standing stones rose against the horizon.

'My mother and my aunt weren't bad people,' Lonnie said. 'They loved me in their way.'

'I bet they did,' I said.

'They always told me that if I went out people would laugh at me. Make fun of me. That's why they kept me inside.'

'Well, that was probably true. People would have made fun of you. Rude people. Ignorant people. I think they might have gotten used to you in the end. Your family tried to protect you, but something tells me they were protecting themselves, too.'

Lonnie was looking at the road. All I could see was the top of his hat, and the hump of his shoulder beneath the red coat.

'When Aisling came, I hid from her. I thought she would run away when she saw me. I would only talk to her from under a sheet. She must have thought I was crazy.'

'She was very hurt by the way you'd been treated, Lonnie,' I said. 'She wanted to do right by you.'

'In the books and stories, there are worlds where all sorts of people live,' Lonnie said with bitterness in his voice, 'and where no one is seen as stupid or weird or strange. Why can't that be the way it is in real life? Why is it that somewhere like Drumlin is the exception rather than the rule?'

'I'm afraid that people are rarely that honourable or open,' I said. 'Most of us fear what is different. It's the same the world over.'

Lonnie climbed over the fence that led to the standing stones, scaling it in three nimble jumps. I followed a little more stiffly. I was constantly amazed at how agile he was.

'The other day, instead of sending Aisling, I went to the shop myself,' Lonnie said. 'I thought everyone was looking at me, but I told myself I was just being stupid, that there was no way I was that interesting or exciting. I got my few bits and pieces and I went to the cash register. There was a girl who couldn't have been more than fifteen or sixteen there, and I could tell straight away that she was barely holding in the laughter. The minute I went past, she burst into a fit of guffaws.'

'I'm sorry, Lonnie,' I said. 'What did you do?'

'I ran. I hightailed it out of there, and I gave Aisling dog's abuse when I got back home for letting me go shopping in the first place. She didn't deserve that, Shane. But I was so angry.'

The stones were in a rough triangle facing east. Lonnie looked out over the rolling glacial landscape. He could easily have been a character from one of the books he so loved.

'Lonnie, the world has dealt you a tough hand,' I said, leaning against one of the rocks. I was wearing a thick leather jacket and a scarf, but there was a sharp wind coming in over the hills and it was chilly. 'People have let you down again and again, and you have every fucking right to be mad as hell. And you know what?'

'What?'

'Giving Aisling an earful, screaming at me every now and again, admitting at news that you're in a shitty mood – it's all right to do that, you know. We're all your friends, and we can take it. You don't have to be the jokey, smart-arsed little guy you pretend to be all the time.'

'If I start letting all that out,' Lonnie said, his voice trembling, his back still to me, 'I'm afraid it might not stop.'

'That's a risk you'll have to take.'

'I'm scared.'

'I know.'

I think he was crying, but he remained where he was, and I did not approach him. If he wished to keep his grief private, that was his privilege.

We stayed in that high place until the sun started to go down, comforted by the vastness of the sky and the immutable wind.

33

'I sit next to Sukie, Max,' Dominic said.

'No. Me.'

'I. Sitting. Next. To. Sukie,' Dominic said and, without missing a beat, sent Max sailing across the room.

'Dominic, no!' Sukie chided him, and went over to see if Max was all right.

'I didn't do it,' Dominic said, crossing his arms over his chest.

Max seemed to be none the worse for his short flight, and he moved to another seat about the table.

This sort of thing had been happening a lot lately. Dominic had become more and more jealous of anyone spending time with, or even around, Sukie. So determined was he about this that he put Max's early histrionics to shame. The problem was that with Dominic reason rarely worked. When he got an idea into his head, nothing would dissuade him or dislodge it.

'Sukie is my girlfriend, Max,' he called across the wide table to his sulking friend.

'She not!' Max said, his heckles well and truly up, now. 'Shane, tell him!'

'Dominic, Sukie is your friend, but she is not your girlfriend.'

'She is, Shane. She tell me.'

'I doubt that very much, Dom,' I said. 'She is your friend, and she likes you a hell of a lot, but she's not your girlfriend. That's a very different sort of friend.'

'I love Sukie, she my girlfriend,' Dominic said pettishly, and laid his head down in his hands.

Sukie had been in the kitchen getting Dominic's and her

own lunch ready. She came back in, carrying their plates, and sat down next to him. He didn't look up.

'What's the matter, Dommy?'

Dominic's voice was muffled by his hands, but I still caught the interchange.

'You my girlfriend, Sukie?'

'Of course I am, poppet.'

I froze. One of the basic principles in dealing with people with special needs – whether that means individuals with intellectual disabilities, or the kind of social retardations that can result from abuse or severe neglect, is the importance of absolute honesty. I did not doubt that Sukie meant nothing by the remark – she saw no harm in this little pretence. Girlfriend could be taken in all sorts of connotations, after all.

The truth was, though, that it was very clear the interpretation Dominic was placing on it, and I didn't like it one little bit. Poor, sweet Dominic was confused enough about this complex, awkward world of ours without adding to his problems. I determined to speak to Sukie about it at the first available opportunity, and get her to put this right. I had no idea exactly how she was going to put it right – as I have already said, Dominic could be very stubborn. But I knew for definite that things *must* be put right.

When lunch was over, I went over to Sukie, and asked her to step into the office with me for a moment. I was, by now, very angry. Sukie may have been inexperienced, but she was far from stupid, had been through a college course and knew the basics of social care very well. The mistake she had made was one I would have expected from someone who had no inkling of how a place like Drumlin worked.

I didn't beat about the bush when the door of the office was closed.

'What are you thinking, Sukie?'

'What do you mean?'

'What have you told Dominic?'

'What?'

'Did you tell him you are his girlfriend?'

'No!'

'I just heard you!'

'What?'

'You know exactly what I'm talking about. Don't mess me around, Sukie. Why did you tell him that?'

Sukie sat down and shook her head in exasperation. 'Come on, Shane, it's only a game. He's such a big old softie, there's no malice in him. Sure, he's like a big, cuddly teddybear.'

'He's a sixteen-year-old boy – a young man – with all the desires and needs of any other kid his age. Except, with Dominic, the ability to understand and channel those feelings is seriously compromised. Today, he tossed Max across the room like he was a soft toy because he wanted to sit next to you. What'll he do next? You've got to set him straight. Right now.'

'Oh for God's sake, lighten up, Shane, will you?' Sukie said. 'I'll break it to him gently. Look, we've got gym this afternoon, so he'll be busy. I'll chat to him tomorrow, okay?'

'What are you going to say?'

'I don't know. Look, I've been dealing with men ever since I grew a pair of tits. I'll sort it out.'

I genuinely wanted to believe her. I really did.

34

Jimmy Simms is a multi-instrumentalist I met and played with occasionally while living in the city, and one day I saw with great delight that he was to perform a gig in the local arts centre. Jimmy is a brilliant musician, a fantastic storyteller, and has such an eclectic style that everyone finds something they like in any show he does. His set ranges from comedy songs concerning two-timing grannies, to serious folk ballads about lost love, to rockabilly numbers about cars and girls. I thought it would be wonderful to bring the group from Drumlin to see him, and I knew he'd be delighted to have them along. Tristan agreed whole-heartedly, and notes were sent around to the various parents and carers to inform them of our intention to bring their loved ones out to see a show.

Everyone was allowed go, and on the night in question we all met at Drumlin, where a little pre-gig party was laid out (we remembered the crispie buns this time). Max was particularly excited. He had never been to a gig before, and in fact rarely went out much in the evenings except to go for a walk or a cycle while it was still reasonably bright. This was a huge treat for him, and he was dressed to the nines in a specially bought shirt and jeans, with his hair gelled to within an inch of its life, and reeking of Brut aftershave.

'You look lovely, Max,' Ricki said.

'I know!' Max grinned.

'Tell her she look nice too,' Elaine barked.

'Look lovely, Ricki,' Max said, suitably chastened.

'Thank you, Max,' Ricki said.

When everyone had eaten, we piled into the minibus, and made our way into town. I had arranged for seats to be reserved for us, and we arrived a little bit early, so the group could have a wander around the various exhibitions of paintings and sculptures that were on show in the centre's three galleries. A small bar served drinks, and, with glasses in hand, and nibbling the odd canapé, our little crew wandered about the beautiful old building, commenting on the art and chatting about the upcoming concert.

When there was around ten minutes to show time, a bell was rung, and we all took our seats. An announcement came over the public address system to let us know where the fire escapes were, and to inform us that there would be a brief intermission during which the bar would be open. Then Jimmy took to the stage.

He is a short barrel of a guy, with a thick head and face of grey wiry hair. From Texas originally, he's been living in Ireland for many years, and plays Irish traditional music as well as any Irish musician I've ever known, but does not limit himself to any particular idiom. He opened the show with an American old-time song, which he played on a beautiful old mandola, and went on from there. Every song was punctuated with stories about his life and times on the road, of the people he had met, of places he had seen, of other musicians he had met and played with and fought with. The first hour or so passed quickly, and at the interval we filed downstairs again.

The group were all in high spirits. Jimmy had welcomed them from the stage as his guests, and they all felt a little bit special that night. I knew some – Max in particular – had been just a shade nervous about coming out, and I could see that, as he ordered a drink from the bar, he had relaxed somewhat. Jimmy had come downstairs and was mingling with the crowd, and then came over to introduce himself to the Drumlin group. I was chatting with him about one of the songs he had done when things went badly wrong. Piecing together the various perspectives on what occurred from Ricki, Elaine, Glen and Max, I think I now have an accurate picture of the chain of events. Dominic, who was right in the middle of the whole thing, always refused to talk about it.

Max had, by now, consumed one or two drinks, and was feeling relaxed and ebullient. Standing in a small group with some of his friends from Drumlin, he was telling a few jokes. Max's idea of a joke is a little different from yours or mine, as it tends not to feature a recognizable punch line, but, for whatever reason, the folk at Drumlin have always found them hilarious.

I have thought back and asked myself if Max was being particularly loud, if he might have been disturbing the people in the room who were not used to him, and for the life of me, I cannot answer the question. It is possible that he was being just a little too noisy, and that someone not accustomed to a person with Down's Syndrome, or with his particular speech defect, might have been disturbed by his conversation. But I do not think that excuses the manner in which such a disturbance, real or imagined, was dealt with.

There were three men standing behind Max, Ricki, Elaine, Glen and Dominic. It seems that one, a tall, well-built guy with a Dublin accent, had turned and said, 'Keep it down there, bud. You're puttin' me off me drinks, here.'

Max had apologized and continued with his story.

'I said turn the volume down,' the man said again, pushing his way between Ricki and Glen, and poking Max in the chest. 'Either you shut up, or I'm goin' to have you sent back to the fuckin' nuthouse, right?'

The man turned on his heel, and went back to his friends.

'Fuckin' spas,' he had said. 'Shouldn't be let out.'

It is hard to determine whether it was this final comment or his general tone of aggression that caused Dominic to see red, but see red he did. In two steps he was beside the loudmouth.

'You not nice,' he said, then drew his fist back and hit him. I didn't see the punch, but I'm told he threw it like a professional with all his weight behind it. The man was lifted off his feet, and landed with a thud flat on his back. By the time he hit the ground, Dominic had returned to Max and the others as if nothing had happened.

Needless to say, we did not see the second half of the show.

No charges were pressed, but we were asked not to bring Dominic back to the arts centre. Jimmy told me afterwards that he thought Dominic was absolutely right to 'punch that arsehole'. I decided it was probably not appropriate to pass that information along, although I secretly agreed with it.

35

Annie was crying.

She wasn't sobbing, or wailing – wasn't, in fact, making any noise at all to signify that she was upset. But tears were streaming down her face as if some internal valve system had sprung a leak.

She had arrived in that morning later than usual, dropped off, she told me, by her cousin Charlie. When I got out to the front door, hoping to meet this famous relative, he was, alas, gone. All I could see was the rear of a battered-looking Fiat 127 as it disappeared into the blue yonder.

It was when I got back inside that I realized how upset the girl was.

'What's wrong, Annie?' I said. 'Tell me what's bothering you.'

She just turned away so she was facing the other direction: if I couldn't see her tears, then maybe I would forget they were there. I wasn't so easily dissuaded.

'Come on, Annie. You and I are too good friends for me to fall for that one.'

I gently turned her back round, and held her there. Sometimes, because I saw her every day, and worked alongside her, I forgot just how beautiful she was. Even with tear-streaked cheeks and a runny nose, she was lovely.

'Did you have a row with your dad, sweetheart? Is that it?'

She shook her head.

'Not Daddy.'

'What is it then?'

In a single motion, Annie collapsed against me, sobbing uncontrollably. It was as if her spine had suddenly been removed and she could no longer support herself.

If this had all been happening in a movie, I would have swept her up in my arms and carried her to a chair, but in real life, things are never as simple as that. Even though she was a slender creature, she still presented a fairly severe dead weight, and I kind of dragged her, still leaning against me, to the library corner and deposited her unceremoniously onto a beanbag.

Beth always ensured that there were plenty of tissues and baby wipes all over the room, as our group was rather prone to accidents involving the entire array of bodily fluids, and I grabbed a handful of tissues and brought them over to the girl, who was now making quite a racket. No one came near us. Getting upset was part and parcel of the Drumlin experience. Everyone did it from time to time, and the need for personal space was always respected – most of the group knew that you needed room to have a really good cry.

When Annie had settled a bit, I tried again.

'Annie, do you want to tell me what's up, or would you like me to get Beth or Millie? Sukie, maybe?'

Annie shook her head. 'Shane friend. Good friend,' she said.

'Yes, I am your friend,' I said. 'You're my oldest friend in Drumlin, aren't you? If it wasn't for you, I wouldn't have come here at all.'

'L'il Liza Jane,' Annie sang through her tears.

'Yeah,' I said. 'That's what we sang, isn't it?'

She covered her face with her hands, and cried again for a time. I just sat there. Sometimes, saying nothing – just being there – is the best thing you can do. I felt Annie would tell me what was wrong when she was ready. I would just have to wait until she had gotten enough of the pain out of her system to be able to find the words.

Suddenly she looked at me and said, 'Charlie fuck.'

I blinked. I am well used to expletives. I work with people who often experience extremes of emotion, and swear words tend to be part and parcel of how they communicate their experiences. It is not unheard of for me to use the odd four-letter word myself. But I had never heard Annie swear, and I found the word ugly coming out of her mouth.

'Did you have a fight with Charlie?'

Annie shook her head. 'No. Charlie fuck.'

I felt a pit opening up inside me, and a terrible coldness beginning to creep up from my toes. 'Did Charlie hurt you, Annie?'

She nodded. 'Hurt inside of me,' she said, placing her hand low on her abdomen. 'He say it "fuck". He say it good. Be like love.'

'But you didn't want him to,' I said quietly. 'Did you?'

'No want,' she said. 'Charlie my friend. Walking and laughing and singing. Not like that. He was in me.'

And then she was crying again.

Tristan looked grim.

Two officers from the local garda station – a male and a female – sat opposite us in the small office at Drumlin. Beth had made up a kind of makeshift bed in the kitchen, and Annie was asleep. I wanted to kill someone, but I was trying to keep it together. Me losing the run of myself would not help anything.

'We go through the correct channels,' Tristan said. 'There is nothing to be gained by going off half-cocked.'

'Ms Kelleher is twenty-seven years old,' the male guard was saying. 'But you say she is intellectually subnormal.'

'Yes.'

'Yet on the file you have just shown me, it says that she has an IQ in the low–average range.'

'Those tests are not always a useful measurement,' Tristan said. 'Annie has what you might call a non-specific form of mental handicap – her functioning is very high in some areas, while it is like that of a small child in others.'

'And she maintains that this cousin of hers raped her?' the female guard asked.

'She did not use those precise words,' I said. 'But she was quite clear that what happened did not occur with her consent. I am not sure she is even capable of giving consent.'

'Yet she has a normal IQ,' the male garda said again.

'Are you going to investigate this matter or not?' Tristan said sharply. 'I have a very upset young lady on my hands, and there is no doubt in my mind that she has been sexually assaulted.'

The two gardaí looked at one another.

'We'll see what we can do,' the woman said.

There was no way to contact William Kelleher.

'They don't have a telephone,' Beth said. 'Any time we need to get information to him, it's by post, or we send letters home with Annie.'

'He probably knew damn well what was going on with that perve,' Valerie said.

'No,' I said. 'He loves Annie. There is no way he would allow this, I can promise you that.'

'What are we going to do then?' Beth said. 'She can't go home.'

'She can stay with me until we hear back from the police,' Tristan said. 'The spare room can be made up.'

'I'll come too,' Beth said. 'She needs to have people around that she knows, just now.'

Tristan nodded. He looked tired and pinched. 'That would be good, Beth.'

My phone rang at around eight that night.

'The police called,' Tristan said, when I picked up.

'And?'

'They said that there is no sign of William out at the old house. They did encounter our man Charlie, who swears that he never touched Annie, although he says she tried to have her way with him.'

190

'That is so fucked up.'

'I know.'

'So what's going to happen?'

'Probably very little. I wish we could reach William.'

'Okay. I'll see you tomorrow,' I said and hung up.

The door to the underground room was open and I went down it and through to the body of the house proper. The first room I came to was a kitchen, which was full of foul dishes. A smell of rancid milk pervaded.

'William? William, it's Shane.'

No answer. I flicked a light switch, which looked like it might have been fitted in the nineteen thirties, but it didn't work. I moved on to the next room, which was where William and I had talked and drank. Charlie was there.

He was sprawled on the couch with bottles of William's home-brewed liquor scattered about. He was dozing when I came in, but woke when he heard my footsteps. Long and skinny, he had dirty-brown hair, and ears that should have been clipped back when he was a child. He wore filthy jeans and a checked shirt which was open to the waist, showing a scrawny, hairless chest.

'You're Charlie,' I said.

'So?'

'I'm Shane Dunphy. From the Drumlin Unit. I work with Annie.'

'I know who you are,' he said. 'She's told me all about you.'

I laughed bitterly. 'She's told me all about you, too.'

He pulled himself upright and, reaching over, poured himself another drink. 'The cops have already been here, man. I told them all I've got to say.'

'Is that right?'

'Yeah. She was all over me, man. "Oh, Charlie, you're my friend, you're my heart," whatever the fuck that means. It got so she was driven' me mad, followin' me about everywhere I went.'

'I thought she was your friend,' I said. 'William told me you understood her better than anyone.'

'Ah, she's okay,' he said, taking a great swallow of poteen. 'I mean, she's fuckin' easy on the eye, man, you can't deny that. You'll forgive a lot when a woman's got a shape like that, y'know what I mean?'

I think he expected me to agree with him. I just stood there, feeling sick, rage building in me with such ferocity, I thought I might actually go mad.

'She'd be always huggin' and kissin' me, and sure it was no bother to cop a sneaky feel. She never noticed. Had me hands all over her, I did.'

He was drunk, and getting drunker by the minute, taking in the poteen like it was water.

'And I bet you got tired of that, didn't you, Charlie?' I asked. 'It's all well and good putting your hands on a girl, but it's like looking at a beautiful place through a dirty window – you're only getting a small part of the experience.'

'Now you're talkin',' he said. 'Here I was, I've got this fuckin' babe right in front of me – and she's a shaggin' retard, man. She's rubbin' her tits in me face, more or less, and she doesn't even know what it's doin' to me. Now, I tried to tell her, tried to explain, but I might as well have been talkin' to meself.'

'So you thought you'd show her.'

'Learnin' by doin'. Exactamondo, my good man.'

'Charlie fuck,' I said.

'That's it. And she fuckin' loved it.'

I walked over and poured myself a drink.

'Help yourself, man.'

'She loved it so much,' I said, downing the burning fluid in two gulps, and pouring another, 'that when you were done, she came to me in tears, so upset she could barely speak. She enjoyed it to such a degree, all she could tell me about was the pain of having you in her. Oh, you did her a real service, you sick bastard.'

Charlie laughed at that.

'Wanted to have a pop at her yourself, did you, compadre? Oh, she was always talkin' about you. You could have been in there, buddy.'

I grabbed him, then.

'You need to get your filthy hide away from here, and never come back,' I said. 'Right now. Are we clear?'

'Fuck you,' he spat back at me, not even struggling. 'I know a good thing when I see it. I'm not goin' anywhere.'

'I'm telling William,' I said. 'I don't know where he is, but I'll find him. When he knows, he'll tear you limb from limb.'

'I'm family. He'll believe me.'

'Annie is more family to him than you are, you fucking scumbag.'

'She's retarded, arsehole,' Charlie cackled. 'No one will take a word she says seriously.'

'I do,' I said. 'I take her seriously.'

He roared with laughter at that.

'What are you going to do? You're a fuckin' nurse or some-thin' on the centre's payroll. If you so much as toss my hair, I'll have you sacked.'

I hit him square in the forehead, and caught him again on the cheekbone before he hit the floor. They were two good punches, and he lay, amid the spilt booze and broken glass, wondering what happened.

I stood over him, feeling better than I had all day.

'You can't get me fired,' I said jubilantly, 'I'm a volunteer.'

PART 9

This Land Belongs to You and Me

The little boy lost in the lonely fen,
Led by the wandering light,
Began to cry, but God, ever nigh,
Appeared like his father, in white.

He kissed the child, and by the hand led,
And to his mother brought,
Who in sorrow pale, through the lonely dale,
The little boy weeping sought.

'The Little Boy Found' by William Blake

36

The day after I confronted Charlie, Dominic almost killed a man.

I was in the unit, setting up the chairs for news, and running through the songs I was going to do for our music session later that day, when I heard screaming coming from outside. At first, I thought it was someone playing and paid no heed, but the urgency and pitch of it seemed so consistent that after a minute or so, I went out to see what was going on. What I saw was almost too horrific to countenance.

Dominic, who was roaring at the top of his voice, had a man by the scruff of the neck with one hand, and was beating him repeatedly with the other about the head and face. Sukie was screaming (despite the fact that Dominic's bellows were louder, hers were at a higher register, and seemed to carry further), and trying to stop him beating the by now unconscious figure, but she was making no progress.

It took me a few seconds to take it all in, and realize that, if something was not done quickly it would be too late for the object of Dominic's wrath. I did the only thing I could think of: I ran across the yard, jumped up on the low wall, and threw myself bodily at Dominic. Luckily, I caught him off guard, and he, I and the poor bloke he'd been pummelling crashed to the ground.

'That's enough, Dominic,' I shouted as I pulled myself to my feet. 'No more!'

'Sukie my girlfriend,' he said, his voice hoarse and thick with tears. 'She mine, okay?'

Tristan had been roused from his office by the commotion, and was pulling the bloodied man aside. Beth had the first-aid box under her arm, and I could hear sirens in the distance.

'What happened?' I asked Sukie, my eyes still on the giant who was sitting on the ground, crying and rocking.

'He was only kissing me goodbye,' the girl said. I could tell she was on the verge of hysteria.

'Boyfriend?' I asked.

'No, not really,' she said. 'I met him at a nightclub last night. He stayed over at my place. Dropped me to work.'

'Sukie. Is. My. Girlfriend,' Dominic said again. 'He not her boyfriend, okay?'

'Shut up!' Sukie shouted at him. 'You shut up, you fucking freak! I am not your girlfriend! I never was and I never will be.'

Dominic began to cry harder. I went over and put my arms round him, and tried to comfort him, but he was inconsolable. Tristan went with him in the police car when they took him away.

'My daddy picking me up at four o'clock, Tristan?' he asked as the door was closed.

'Maybe not today, Dominic,' Tristan said.

'I 'fraid, Tristan,' Dominic said urgently: 'I wants my daddy, 'kay?'

I turned away, my eyes blind with tears, the story Annie had told on my first day at Drumlin coming jarringly back to me. If Dominic was ever lost, he was then. And it didn't look like this lost little boy would find his happily ever after.

37

It was a sedate and solemn group at news the following day.

'Where Dominic?' Max wanted to know.

'He is in a hospital, at the moment,' Tristan said. 'He is a little bit upset, and when he was in the police station he had quite a severe seizure. His mum and dad both thought it might be better for him to stay there until he was feeling better.'

Beth said nothing. Her eyes were red, and she kept sniffing and wiping at her nose.

'Where's Sukie?' Ricki asked the next question that was on everyone's mind.

'Sukie won't be coming back to Drumlin,' Tristan admitted. 'She feels that she doesn't really fit in, and she's resigned from her job here.'

'Miss Sukie,' Max said, sighing.

'I miss Dominic,' Ricki said.

'I miss Annie,' Glen said.

'Where is Annie?' I asked Tristan, when news was over and I had a moment with him by myself.

'William called for her early this morning.'

'How did he know she was with you?'

'The police told him,' Tristan said. 'Apparently he turned up at the station looking for his daughter in the middle of the night.'

'What brought him there?'

'God knows,' Tristan said. 'They told me that he was in quite a state. Seemed to think she was hurt, or something.'

I nodded. It made as much sense as anything.

'How's she doing, then?'

'Better now she's with her father.'

'Did you tell him about Charlie?'

'I didn't have to,' Tristan said. 'He informed me that the gentleman in question had moved on, and would not be coming back. Whatever that means.'

'Tristan, I couldn't give a damn.'

'My sentiments precisely.'

38

The next time I saw Annie was three weeks later. Lonnie and I were walking on the mountain, a habit we had come to treasure. We crossed a field of silver-frosted grass, and there she was, dancing across the frigid ground to a tune neither of us could hear. If she saw us, she gave no indication, and passed across our line of vision, heading for a cluster of ash two hundred yards to our left. In a minute, she was gone.

'She looks better,' Lonnie said.

He had gotten a haircut, and was wearing a baseball cap, a leather jacket and jeans. He looked good, too.

'What happened to her will take time to heal,' I said, 'but I think she's in the right place for that healing to occur. This is where she loves, and I don't think her dad will ever again leave her unsupervised like he did.'

'Don't be too hard on him,' Lonnie said. 'How could he have known what that bollix was after?'

'You're right, I know,' I said. 'I'm still sore over it all, I suppose.'

'That's okay,' Lonnie said. 'You love her, too.'

'We all do,' I said.

'Yeah.'

We continued our progress over the icy, rocky earth.

'So how are you doing these days?' I asked.

'Up and down,' Lonnie admitted.

'And today?'

'Mostly up.'

He looked at me out of the corner of his eye.

'No jokes about that? "How high up can someone like me actually get," maybe?'

'Naw,' I said. 'I shouldn't have made those gags in the first place.'

'I gave back in spades.'

'It wasn't kind,' I said. 'You deserved better.'

He patted me on the arm. 'We were both learning, I reckon.'

'Learning what?'

'How to be friends with one another,' he said.

The field ended in a line of blackthorn trees, beyond which the land opened up like a picture book. We could see for miles in every direction.

'Drumlin isn't the same lately, is it?' Lonnie said, as we drank in the view. 'Since everything happened.'

'No,' I admitted. 'But Tristan said to me, a year ago now, that the world doesn't stop at the door of the unit. I suppose it just decided to stop waiting on the mat and came on in.'

'It was kind of magic there for a while, though,' he said. 'We had some fun.'

'We'll have more,' I said. 'We'll just have to start over.'

'Do you want to?' Lonnie asked.

'I don't have anything better to do,' I said.

'Me neither.'

And we started to walk back to the warmth of the cottage.

Afterword

Little Boy Lost is a book about new beginnings. It recounts a time in my career when it felt very much as though I was learning to be a care worker almost from scratch, when every step forward seemed painstaking and ridiculously difficult. Yet it was also a time of inexpressible joy. Tristan Fowler, or at least the man upon whom I based him, remains a dear and loyal friend to me to this day. He has taught me more about acceptance and the true meaning of integration than anyone else I have ever known.

I say without any shame that when I ran away to the country, I was completely broken. Drumlin and the amazing people there put me back together again. That all their stories are bittersweet should not be a sign of any kind of failure on their part or on anyone else's. Life is just like that.

I know that some readers will consider it, particularly during these times of economic crisis, deeply foolhardy to wish to work on a voluntary basis when money is being laid on the table. You will have to take my word that, at that time in my career I really did not believe that I would stick the job on offer for more than a few weeks. I felt something would happen to send me running again, and I would then be letting these people, whom I already cared a great deal about, down. I could not stand the idea of carrying more guilt around with me. Volunteering seemed the best option. By signing nothing and promising less, I was not tied, either legally or morally. It was as much as I could cope with.

Dominic never came out of the psychiatric hospital where he was placed after the incidents described here. He died there as a result of a severe epileptic seizure. I think of him often with deep sadness, but also great fondness. He was a gentle, sweet-natured, wonderful person, who was simply too trusting for this world.

Reading this book and seeing the number of occasions where Dominic became violent, I expect some of you are questioning my calling him 'gentle', and that is understandable. You must remember that Dominic was operating, to all intents and purposes, at the level of a toddler. Children are physical – when a baby does not want a toy or to eat his dinner, he throws that item out of the pram or away from the high chair. Dominic responded to adversity in a similar way. He had no concept of his strength or of the fact that a table might do some damage if you happened to be in its flight path. He never meant any harm by his actions. He was locked away because of the terrible fear that the roller-coaster of emotions he was falling prey to were becoming too much for him to cope with.

I miss him greatly. He was as true a friend as I have ever had.

I never saw Sukie again. I hope that I have not represented her cruelly in this book, because, in reality, the mistakes she made are commonplace enough. I cannot recall how many times I have encountered qualified staff at day-care centres telling adults with intellectual disabilities that yes, they are their boyfriends/girlfriends, or how many times I have seen girls going to work in settings – from pre-schools up to nursing homes for the elderly – dressed as if they are going out partying.

In the case of Sukie, things ended very badly indeed, yet in the vast majority of cases things just muddle along, usually with a very confused or deeply frustrated population of clients. This is, in actuality, simply lazy care work. The appropriate answer to: 'Are you my girlfriend/boyfriend?' is 'No, I like you very much, but I am your friend.' It is simple, truthful and in no way open to misinterpretation. Sukie did many things right when she was at Drumlin, and through a little investigation, I discovered that she now runs a youth centre in the south-west of Ireland. I wish her well.

Annie is still around. I see her from time to time, and she always makes me smile. The pain of her experiences with Charlie are long forgotten. She finds the world too rich a place to waste on such sadness.

The question the police asked when we discussed Annie with them is a common one in the case of people with learning disabilities: how can someone who is technically just as bright as most 'normal' people be intellectually disabled? The reality is that Annie is quite an intelligent young woman, and a very gifted artist. Yet the way she experiences the world is very different to the way you or I do, and she has difficulty with many things – not least being communication.

I often wonder if the term 'disability' is an appropriate way of thinking about people like my friends in Drumlin at all. I really believe they are just different. And I have always thought that difference is something we should celebrate rather than hide away or try to mould into an image of conformity.

Yet Annie is another person for whom the world is just too difficult a place. She is more at home on her mountain, in the fields and the woods and the high places. And even that is disappearing. I have, of late, come to think of her as an endangered species whose habitat is being gradually eroded by developers and builders. There is a large housing estate not a mile from her home now, and a factory is to be built later this year where her woods are situated.

Lonnie continued to attend Drumlin, more as a member of staff than as a client (the lines are often blurred, as sometimes seemed natural there) until his death, as a result of a congenital heart problem, at the age of forty-two. Of my friend I can say that he took life on his own terms and did not look back. He died a contented and well-loved man.

There is a term in disability studies: disability activism. It describes individuals with disabilities who see their situation as a political position, and campaign for rights and access and integration. A large part of their stance is that having a disability is something not to be ashamed of but should be a source of pride. Lonnie had never heard of disability activism yet, he was, in his own peculiar way, quite proud to be a dwarf. He was aware that people found the way he looked funny, and he understood that he was unusual in a world that values blandness, but nevertheless, he learned to love himself. He made a point of going to the shops, of going about his business in the small town close to where he lived, and even though people still stared and mocked him from time to time, he was a big enough person to realize that the problem was not his, but theirs. It is a grave pity that so many of those ignorant people could not understand that basic truth.

Beth Singleton left Drumlin – and Tristan Fowler – several years after the events described in this book. She went back to nursing, and on the odd occasion our paths cross, she always reports that she is very happy.

And maybe she is.

He just wanted a decent book to read ...

Not too much to ask, is it? It was in 1935 when Allen Lane, Managing Director of Bodley Head Publishers, stood on a platform at Exeter railway station looking for something good to read on his journey back to London. His choice was limited to popular magazines and poor-quality paperbacks – the same choice faced every day by the vast majority of readers, few of whom could afford hardbacks. Lane's disappointment and subsequent anger at the range of books generally available led him to found a company – and change the world.

'We believed in the existence in this country of a vast reading public for intelligent books at a low price, and staked everything on it'
Sir Allen Lane, 1902–1970, founder of Penguin Books

The quality paperback had arrived – and not just in bookshops. Lane was adamant that his Penguins should appear in chain stores and tobacconists, and should cost no more than a packet of cigarettes.

Reading habits (and cigarette prices) have changed since 1935, but Penguin still believes in publishing the best books for everybody to enjoy. We still believe that good design costs no more than bad design, and we still believe that quality books published passionately and responsibly make the world a better place.

So wherever you see the little bird – whether it's on a piece of prize-winning literary fiction or a celebrity autobiography, political tour de force or historical masterpiece, a serial-killer thriller, reference book, world classic or a piece of pure escapism – you can bet that it represents the very best that the genre has to offer.

Whatever you like to read – trust Penguin.